Career Change
In A Week

Patricia Scudamore and Hilton Catt have many years' experience of working in recruitment, enabling them to bring the perspective of both employer and candidate. They have written over 25 books based on their experience of what it takes to make careers work in today's rapidly changing and uncertain world. They were among the first to embrace the idea of people taking on the job of managing their own careers as opposed to leaving it to employers to do the thinking for them. They have seen for themselves the richness and diversity modern careers can offer and one of the central themes in their work is exploiting this richness and diversity to the full. They have written a number of other books in the Teach Yourself series. You can visit their website at scudamorecatt.com and their blog site at patriciascudamorehiltoncatt.com

Teach® Yourself

Career Change In A Week

Patricia Scudamore &
Hilton Catt

First published in Great Britain in 2012 by Hodder & Stoughton. An Hachette UK company.

This revised, updated edition published in 2016 by John Murray Learning

Copyright © Pat Scudamore and Hilton Catt 2012, 2016

British Library Cataloguing in Publication Data: a catalogue record for this title is available from the British Library.

Library of Congress Catalog Card Number: on file.

Paperback ISBN 978 1 473 60770 5

Ebook ISBN 978 1 444 18631 4

1

Typeset by Cenveo® Publisher Services.

Printed and bound in Great Britain by CPI Group (UK) Ltd., Croydon, CR0 4YY.

John Murray Learning policy is to use papers that are natural, renewable and recyclable products and made from wood grown in sustainable forests. The logging and manufacturing processes are expected to conform to the environmental regulations of the country of origin.

John Murray Learning
Carmelite House
50 Victoria Embankment
London EC4Y 0DZ
www.hodder.co.uk

Also available in ebook

Contents

Introduction

Writing on the subject of career changes ten years ago, we observed that the days of spending all our working lives in one career might already be over. Nothing since then has caused us to revise this opinion. Done properly, however, a change of career can be a rewarding and exhilarating experience and one you should never shrink from, particularly if the alternative is underachieving, stagnating in a dead-end job or doing work you no longer find interesting. This book teaches you all you need to know about crossing the bridge from one career to another.

The world in which we have to work and make a living has, if anything, become even more difficult than it was a decade ago. Most of us will therefore probably have to face the prospect of moving into a completely new field of work at some stage. Our jobs may come to an end as a result of changing work patterns or technological change; we may want more – or less – from our jobs than we are getting, or we may just decide that the career that beckoned at the start of our working life has become less appealing ten or more years on.

A recurring question for many people in organizations is how long they have before the next headcount slash comes round. Whatever the driving force happens to be – a recession, spending cuts, the need to make a bigger return for shareholders – the end result is redundancy. Being made redundant a few times may be all part of life's rich pattern but, when it keeps happening, people can arrive at the stage where they feel they've had enough. They ask themselves what's there for them in the long term. Will it be more of the same? Their thoughts turn to what else they could do, what new career they could move into, what's out there that could get them out of the never-ending cycle of uncertainty they seem to be in.

Technological advances and new ways of doing things have wiped some careers off the map altogether, so the people in them have no choice other than to find something else. We also have greater expectations of our jobs. We set our sights higher and place a greater value on the quality of our lives. We all want something better, something more fulfilling, something we find more enjoyable – or simply something that pays us more. Since we are now living and working longer (a trend set to continue), what we're doing now may not be what we want to do as we get older. On the supply side, there's a lot more opportunity out there, not just in the range and diversity of careers available but also the easier access to them, courtesy of greater flexibility in the job market and better learning opportunities.

This book is broken down into seven short lessons, one for each day of the week. It starts by putting your ideas to the test to see whether they are viable or not. Then, if they are, it goes on to show you what you need to do to move your plan from an outline in your head to a reality. Sometimes the challenges you'll face will be tough ones, but throughout the book you'll find practical advice and tips to help you when you get stuck and need to find a way forward.

Pat Scudamore & Hilton Catt

SUNDAY

Starting off

There are two different types of career change and it's important at the outset to know which category you fit into. Then you will need to identify the skills, qualifications and know-how you can take with you into your new career (your 'transferable talents'). Today you'll learn how these transferable talents will help you when it comes to realizing your ambitions.

While changing your career might be the right step to take, it's important to examine your commitment before you start, so that lack of it doesn't become the reason for giving up. Today we'll address the following questions:

- Is there a demand for people in the career you've set your heart on? Are there going to be jobs at the end of it?
- Can you do the job? Will employers view you as someone suitable?
- Are you engaging with reality? Does the new career offer what you think it will offer? Are there snags you may not have considered?
- Do you have the staying power to see it through?

See where you're coming from

In most cases, people change careers for one of two reasons. You may be forced to change career through no choice of your own, or you may be freely choosing to change direction because you have a vision of something better.

The first reason for changing career may arise as the result of a situation not of your choosing. You may experience the onset of a disabling medical condition or lose your driving licence, or you may find that you are in a role where technology has moved forward or markets have changed so that there is no longer a call for your line of work.

Key points to pick out with forced career changes are these:

- The compulsion to alter direction is driven by external events.
- Your job is under threat (or will be shortly).
- You have no fixed ideas about what you want to do next.

The second reason for changing career is a visionary one, and one that you are freely choosing to make. You see something better at the end of it, such as greater job satisfaction, less stress or the ability to earn more money.

Important points to pick out here are these:

- The career change is driven by a dream (the vision).
- The job you're doing currently is probably safe.
- Your ideas about what you want to do next tend to be fixed.

Identifying your transferable talents

You will already have a bank of skills and experience, some of which will be useful to you in your new career. Beside the obvious, core skills of your current job, you will usually find that you possess more in the way of transferable talents than you first think. It's important to identify all your talents because they will be the facilitators when it comes to making your change of career.

> ## Case study: Ayesha
>
> Ayesha is a secretary/PA who wants to become an IT teacher. She sees teaching as a more rewarding career than running round her boss all day and covering for his mistakes. She would also get more holiday and more time to spend with her family.
>
> Because of her job, which includes working with many of the leading brands of software, Ayesha already has an excellent range of IT skills. What's more, these skills lend themselves directly to the new career she has chosen. She also sees that she has other attributes that mark her out as someone suitable to teach IT. She is good at organizing herself, thinking on her feet and working to deadlines. Like most PAs, she knows what she can and can't say without stepping over sensitive boundaries.

Does the plan hold together?

The first thing to assess is whether your ideas are viable or not. Will the new career you've set your sights on deliver what you think it is going to deliver or will it turn out to be a costly disappointment? Here are some questions to ask yourself.

1 **Will there be a job at the end of it?**
   Are there jobs waiting out there or are the opportunities scarce? You also need to consider the fact that, as a novice,

it will be harder for you to find openings. The jobs we're talking about therefore need to be in plentiful supply.

> ## Warning
>
> Too many people embark on plans to change their careers without giving proper consideration to the job market. They press on regardless, and then find out – when they have gone through all the hard bits – that they can't get a job. Usually, they end up going back to their old career. In short, they achieve nothing, except for chalking up a lot of negative experiences.

2 Is there evidence of market demand?

You can't beat the market and, in this respect, the job market is the same as any other. Before you set off on your plan to change careers, you need to look for hard evidence that someone out there is going to want you at the end of it. Where do you look for this evidence, bearing in mind that the sector of the job market you want to find out about could be completely new to you?

- A quick and relatively easy place to start is by scanning the job ads in newspapers and periodicals and on websites.
- Talk to a few recruitment consultants (employment agencies), especially those who specialize in the sector of the market on which you have set your sights.
- Talk to anyone else you know who may have some first-hand knowledge of job market conditions in the line of work that interests you.
- See at the same time whether you can find out more from these sources about what employers want and what you could expect to earn (a) as a beginner and (b) when you've got more experience.

3 Do I fit the specification?

Ditching the job in an insurance office that has become boring and going off to play professional football sounds like a brilliant idea. Not only is there all the money professional footballers can make but also there's the adulation of the fans when you score the winning goal and the glitzy lifestyle that goes with being a celebrity. But what if you're not physically built for contact sports? What if you're no good when it comes to kicking a ball?

Fortunately for most of us, we have a built-in mechanism for picking up when we don't have what it takes to do certain jobs. We don't have the right skills, we haven't got the right background or our qualifications are completely wrong. A voice inside tells us that it's not just a case of going off on a course to make up for our shortcomings. We're just not suitable, and that's that.

Sometimes, however, these mismatches are less obvious. One of the big problems here is that the assessment of our suitability is one we're making ourselves. So one of the further purposes of studying job ads and talking to people in the know is to see if we meet the specification.

4 Am I dealing with reality?

This is a major issue for anyone considering a change of career. What do you really know about the line of work you've set your sights on and is the information you're relying on accurate? It's important to engage with reality. In particular, don't rely on uninformed and/or prejudiced views. All careers have plus and minus points, so make sure that you're looking at both.

TIP *Take any suggestion that a certain career could land you a soft number with a huge pinch of salt! Soft numbers aren't in great supply any more – or, at least, that's our experience.*

A career in sales: the myth and the reality

Sales to some people means getting dressed up in your best clothes and going out to see customers. Even better, you get to drive round in a company car and you don't have the boss breathing down your neck all day. What's more, you see the world on your travels and it costs you nothing because you can claim it all back on expenses.

Now anyone who has worked in sales will tell you straight away that this is not the way it is. They will tell you what life is really like when you have to work to a call plan and how it's usually you who gets it in the neck when the promises haven't been met or the services haven't been delivered. They will tell you, too, how long they have to spend every night sitting in front of the computer just to keep their reporting up to date and about the way this intrudes into their home life.

Checking out the reality

How do you find out what it's like – really like – to work in the career you would like to get into? The obvious way is to talk to people who have spent time in the career (the nearer the sharp end, the better).

- Try to talk to more than one person (in all walks of life there are individuals with chips on their shoulders who will have a biased view).
- If you don't know anyone, try tapping into your friends/family/professional networks.

SUNDAY

MONDAY

TUESDAY

WEDNESDAY

THURSDAY

FRIDAY

SATURDAY

- Failing this, see whether there is a professional body that could put you on to someone to talk to.
- Ask people what they enjoy about the work as well as the parts they find difficult and challenging – that is, get an all-round view.
- Ask them if they have any advice for a newcomer.

Toe-dipping

There is no better way of finding out more about a career and what it involves than by getting in there and experiencing it at first hand. However, testing the temperature of the water by dipping your toe in first isn't easy when you've got a day job.

Getting time off work to go on a toe-dipping expedition won't be an issue if your name is on a redundancy list. But if you're working full time in a job and you don't want your employer to know about your plan to change careers, you may need to book a few days' holiday.

It may be possible to try out some careers without it interfering with your day job. Ayesha, for example, could find work as an IT teacher in the evenings. In fact, she could run being a secretary/ PA and being an IT teacher in parallel for a while. With the spread of part-time work and job shares, there is increased opportunity for working in two careers at the same time. It is an arrangement you can keep going for as long as you like. It is also a good way of trying out a new career before you commit everything to it.

Identifying bad ideas

As we have seen, not all our ideas are good ones and we've been looking at ways of identifying those that don't stand up. However, some ideas need to be given even greater scrutiny. They include:

- ideas you have on the last day of your holiday
- ideas you have over a glass of wine

- ideas that form after a bad day at work or when the boss is giving you a hard time.

We could go on with this list, but you will have got the message to be careful about going off on wild flights of fancy when you may be viewing life through rose-tinted spectacles or you haven't really got your feet on the ground. The acid test of any idea is what it looks like over a period of time (on bad as well as good days). This is why ideas that evolve are usually better than those that suddenly pop into your head.

Staying power

Changing careers is all about moving the goalposts in big ways. You'll feel a buzz of excitement but at the same time you'll experience a feeling of trepidation because you are taking a step into the unknown. What is certain, though, is that the path you're setting off on won't be a smooth one. It will have its ups and downs and you could find some of the downs challenging. You need to be sure, therefore, that you're 100 per cent serious about what you're seeking to do. Put another way, irrespective of how well your ideas stack up, anything you feel only half-hearted about is never going to work.

You need not just commitment but commitment over what could be long periods (years in some cases). Only you know the answers here. But if the flame you're carrying round inside isn't burning as brightly as it once was, then it's time to ask questions.

Examining your options

One feature of changing careers is that people tend to consider only a limited range of options. Indeed, where the driving force is visionary, it is not unusual to find the list of options confined to one. For example, they want to work in human resources management and nothing else will do – end of discussion.

While this is all well and good, it can (and does) cause problems.

● **Forced career changes**
   When the clock is ticking against you, it makes sense to have as many irons in the fire as possible. Pursuing a small number of options means that, if none of them works out, you'll probably find yourself out of a job.

● **Visionary career changes**
   You could find that you start getting signs that you've made the wrong choice. For example, if you realize you've not got what it takes to be a human resources manager, where does this leave you? Your dream lies in pieces, so what do you do now? Do you resign yourself to staying in the career you've started to find boring? Do you carry on underachieving?

It's important always to look at all the options. Start with your transferable talents and see how many careers you can come up with where your transferable talents would give you a starting point (make a list). If you're working to a deadline because of a forced career change, get going with *all* the options.

Consider all your options. Start with Plan A then, if it doesn't work out, move on to Plan B. Always have a Plan B and even a Plan C, D and E up your sleeve.

The modern job market

This is where the world is on your side. Though it can be difficult at times, today's job market has far more opportunities for people who want to change their careers than has ever been the case in the past. Therefore, as part of examining your full range of options, make it your business to find out what's going on out there. See where someone with your talents could, with a little ingenuity, carve out openings for themselves. You will find that there are many paths for you to choose from, not just one or two.

Summary

Today you looked at the stops and checks you need to have in place to act as a restraint against charging off on a career change that you might later regret. You learned how to test the strength of your ideas by examining what call there is for new entrants into the career you have chosen.

You asked probing questions about what the work will involve, to help you make sure that it is everything you think it is going to be and to see where flights of fancy might have taken over and prevented you from engaging with reality. Some changes of career will be within your reach whereas others won't; it is important to put a clear line between the two.

You also learned to focus on your transferable talents – your biggest assets when it comes to realizing career-change ambitions. Identify how many new careers you can apply them to so that you're not in the position of having a choice of one. In doing this, you'll be able to view the world as your oyster – a place where you can go out and pick and choose.

SUNDAY

MONDAY

TUESDAY

WEDNESDAY

THURSDAY

FRIDAY

SATURDAY

Fact-check [answers at the back]

1. Which of these is a forced career change?
   a) Doing an office job you find boring and deciding you'd like to work with animals ❑
   b) Working in a career involving long trips overseas, then finding you're left with sole responsibility for the care of two small children ❑
   c) Being sacked for something you've done wrong ❑
   d) Being in a career for over 30 years and wanting to do something different, preferably with reduced hours ❑

2. Which of these isn't a visionary career change?
   a) Leaving a job for which there's no longer a call because computers now do the work ❑
   b) Wanting to get out of the rat race and go off and sell ice cream on the beach ❑
   c) Feeling disillusioned with your career after you've been turned down for promotion four times ❑
   d) Winning a talent competition and being told by your friends to pack in your career in retail and try your luck in a boy/girl band ❑

3. What is a transferable talent?
   a) Any skill or attribute you have ❑
   b) A skill or attribute that lends itself to the career you are considering ❑
   c) A skill or other attribute that commands a specially high salary ❑
   d) A skill that will get you a job anywhere in the world ❑

4. Why are transferable talents important?
   a) They are recognized internationally ❑
   b) They will help facilitate your change of career ❑
   c) They are what mark you out as someone who is above average ❑
   d) They show that you have skills that are up to date ❑

5. Which of these is important when you're considering a change of career?
   a) You'll find a job at the end of it ❑
   b) You're choosing a career where employers won't see you as a misfit ❑
   c) You find out first what the work involves ❑
   d) All of the above ❑

6. Who's in the best position to know whether you have enough staying power to see your project through?
a) Your boss ❑
b) Your best friend ❑
c) A professional careers adviser ❑
d) You ❑

7. Which of these career change plans stands the best chance of going the course?
a) One that gets you away from the hassle you have to put up with now ❑
b) One that comes into your head when you're lying on the beach ❑
c) One that evolves over a period of time ❑
d) One you think about when you're feeling angry with the boss ❑

8. Why is it important to look at all the options?
a) To make sure that you're seeing the full range of opportunities open to you ❑
b) To help your self-esteem ❑
c) It's good mental exercise ❑
d) It might make you think twice ❑

9. What should you do if you get negative feedback about a change of career you've been considering for some time (feedback that takes you by surprise)?
a) Stop in your tracks ❑
b) Carry on regardless ❑
c) Take some more soundings ❑
d) Shelve the idea for six months ❑

10. What is toe-dipping?
a) A new form of beauty therapy ❑
b) Taking the chance to try out a new career before you commit yourself fully to the idea ❑
c) Going on holiday and using the break to think through your options more carefully ❑
d) Projects that fail due to lack of enthusiasm ❑

MONDAY

Assessing the risks

A daunting aspect of any planned career change is that no one is underwriting you and your big idea to do something different. Even when you've done the soul-searching, satisfied yourself that your plan is viable and convinced yourself that you've got the staying power to see it through, it's likely that you'll still have some lingering doubts. What if it all goes wrong? What could the fallout be for you and those who depend on you?

Thoughts like these stop many people in their tracks. What lies ahead is unknown territory and this in itself is enough to put them off. Perfectly well-thought-out plans to move into a new career then go no further, and, in many cases, this is a pity.

Today we will focus on assessing the risks of your career-change plan. You will learn how to:

- view risk properly – the upsides and downsides
- assess your capacity to take risks
- quantify the risks
- work out how to finance your plan
- keep your finances afloat by adjusting outgoings, taking on borrowings and/or supplementing income with part-time work
- ensure that spouses/partners/other family members will offer support.

The upsides and downsides

Risk always has two sides to it – an upside and a downside.

The upsides

These are the things you're going to get out of making the move into your new career. They may include a more secure job in a field of work where you won't be under the constant threat of redundancy, less stress, more job satisfaction, access to higher earnings or better learning opportunities – whatever it is that's driving you.

The downsides

These are the problems that might arise if the plan goes wrong. You could be left with the job of picking up the pieces, which may prove difficult.

If your need to make a change of career has come about because, for example, jobs in your line of work are no longer available where you live or because your doctor has told you to find something different, your situation falls under the heading of a forced career change. You don't therefore have the option of carrying on in the career you're in now, so your view of risk (the downside) will be very different from that of someone operating from a more secure standpoint. See Friday's chapter for more about forced career changes.

Assessing your capacity to take risks

When it comes to taking risks that could have a major impact on your earnings, if you have a mortgage to pay and other financial commitments, you will not be in as strong a position as someone who is footloose, fancy-free and comes with no strings attached. In short, your capacity to take risks is linked to your personal circumstances. Two people with exactly the same ambitions could be looking at very different sets of downsides because of what else is going on in their lives. John A who has a wife and two small children to support along with bills to pay each month will need to take a more cautious view than Jane B who lives at home with her well-off parents.

Since capacity to take risks varies from one individual to the next, you'll need to work out for yourself where you come on the scale. Are you a John A or a Jane B or somewhere in between?

What are the risks?

Let's start with the premise that we don't get far in life without taking risks. Every time we change jobs we take a risk but, if we didn't – if we stayed in the job where we're underachieving or being underpaid – we would end up stagnating, or worse. The same can be said for changing careers. Yes, there's a big potential downside in terms of risks but equally there's a big downside to staying in a career that, for example, no longer interests you or in one where you've lost confidence in its ability to provide you with a secure future.

What this illustrates is that to assess risk properly you need to look at *both* the upsides and the downsides then see how they compare. If the upsides look good enough, then, instead of letting the downsides put you off, see what you can do to manage them. On the other hand, if the upsides are inconsequential, then think again, because the risk may not be worth it.

The two biggest downsides for anyone considering a change of career are:

- going back to **being a beginner** in a completely fresh field of work
- the **reduction in earnings** that usually goes with this.

For most people the biggest of these is coming face to face with the harsh reality of having to live on less. Is it something you can afford to do or is it the 'kiss of death' as far as your ideas of changing career are concerned?

As we have seen, our attitudes to risk are linked to our personal circumstances. If we don't have mouths to feed or a mortgage to pay, we will take a very different view from someone who has. Indeed, if you have financial commitments, you will feel understandably nervous about embarking on a course of action that could put you closer to (or even below) the breadline, and you may even start to feel that 'this isn't for me'.

The business model

It may be helpful to see your move into a new career as rather like starting up a new business. At first, the business won't be bringing in much money, so you allow for this by seeking sources of finance to see you through.

Using savings

With **visionary** career changes, where time is on your side, you can save up some money before giving your project the green light. Saving – building up funds for the start-up period of your new career – is good for a number of reasons:

1 **It attaches a proper sense of importance to your project.** It's a way of proving to yourself that you're serious.
2 **It gets you into a good habit.** Not having all your disposable income available for spending conditions you for the period ahead, when you may have to tighten your belt out of necessity.
3 **It inspires confidence in you and others.** Putting your project on a proper financial footing helps make it more convincing to you and to anyone else with whom you may need to share your dreams.
4 **It reduces fear.** Knowing that you will have a financial cushion to protect you against any setbacks that may come along helps to dispel some of the fear of the unknown.

Where saving is difficult

What if you don't have enough disposable income to make regular contributions to a savings plan? What if your incomings and outgoings are so finely balanced that there is nothing left over at the end of each month?

If you really are in this position and not overspending on items you can cut back on, then there are three messages:

● Don't expect a change of career to be painless. Go back to yesterday's chapter and reread all we had to say about commitment and staying power.
● Even if your finances are tight, still see what you can do to put a little aside every month. Even with small amounts of money, regular savings soon build up. It may mean delaying your project for a while but this is infinitely better than scrapping it altogether or, worse still, setting off without sufficient funding and then finding that you run into trouble.
● Fortunately, there are other ways of underwriting career changes apart from out of savings.

Do your sums

Let's look now at how much money you're going to need to fund your change of career. First, we have to estimate the cost. To work out the sums, we need to know the answers to the following questions:

1 What kind of reduction in earnings will your change of career involve?
2 How long will it take you to get back to the level of earnings you enjoyed previously?
3 Are there any other costs – for example, the costs associated with going on a course or getting additional qualifications?

If you have done your homework and followed the steps outlined yesterday, you will already have all the information you need at your fingertips. You will now be able to work out a rough projection of what it is going to cost to change careers. At first, you may find the figures frightening, but console yourself with the thought that being realistic is far better than proceeding with the false idea that you can do it all on a shoestring.

Financial empowerment

Let's now take a look at those big fixed costs that are a central part of most people's personal finances. There are ways to reduce them in the short term so that you can spend the next few years bedding yourself into your new career without being undermined by financial worries. For example, you can consider:

- reducing your mortgage repayments for however long it is going to take to get your earning power back
- taking a holiday from making contributions to your personal pension plan.

In other words, see what you can do to make your finances more **flexible** and more capable of responding to ups and downs in your earnings.

Taking on short-term borrowings

This is where a lot of people, understandably, start to get nervous. Borrowing money (for example, by getting a loan from the bank) has connotations many of us don't like. It is, after all, going into debt and, rightly, our inbuilt warning bells start to ring out whenever the idea is mentioned.

However, going back to the analogy of starting up a new business, it is perfectly normal to find that the start-up capital a business needs is drawn from a mix of shareholders' funds and borrowings. Failing to provide sufficient capital can result in a business foundering, not because of its performance but because it runs out of money.

Part-time working

Getting a part-time job is another way of supplementing your earnings. The flexible workforce, as it is known, has gone through an unprecedented period of growth in recent years. As businesses have sought to make themselves more responsive to fluctuations in demand for their products or services, there has been an upsurge in the demand for people on temporary or short-term contracts of one kind or another, including people who work part time.

Here are some guidelines for how to source part-time work that will help you make ends meet while you are finding your feet in a new career:

- Establish what hours you can work, taking into account the demands of your job/studies and the need to spend time

SUNDAY

MONDAY

TUESDAY

WEDNESDAY

THURSDAY

FRIDAY

SATURDAY

with your family. Don't pretend that you can work all hours (e.g. half the night) because, even if you start, you won't be able to keep it up.

- Identify any skills you may have which lend themselves to part-time work. For example, an ability to ten-finger touch-type may have more bearing on your ability to source part-time work than, say, your skills as a manager.
- Apart from scanning the jobs ads in the local press, talk to a few employment agencies (personal recommendation is a good way of finding the right ones). Tell them what you can do and the hours you can work. Agencies have cornered most of the market for part-time temporary work and they offer what is probably your best chance of finding something suitable.
- Tap into your professional network. Is there anyone you know who could put you on to a part-time job?

When you find a part-time job, never let it get in the way of your new career. If conflict arises, always be clear which you put first.

Using your partner's earnings

Domestic ties are often seen as a handicap when it comes to realizing ambitions such as changing career. The reasons for this including the following:

- They inhibit your ability to take risks. They make you think twice.
- You don't have a free hand in choosing the path you want to follow. You have to take the views of others into account.

However, being in a relationship and having the support of a family can also be a source of strength. People in permanent relationships also have the ability to share the responsibility for paying the bills. Your partner can get a job or extend the hours they work to increase the family income.

Step back to step forward

Keep in mind that the step back in your earnings is likely to be a temporary one because, at some stage, you will move from being a raw beginner to someone with experience who can command a better salary. Coupled with the fact that you will be doing work you want to do, the step back will be what enables you to make a giant leap forward. It is important for you to see it in this way.

Gaining moral support

Changing careers is a time in your life when you will need the full support and understanding of all those who share your life and depend on you. The path ahead won't be easy and, even if it all goes relatively smoothly, there will still be some bleak moments. Here is where a strongly supportive partner can be a great asset, especially when you're having doubts about whether you're doing the right thing. What you need to do, though, is make great efforts to keep your partner onside, by:

● communicating your ideas right from the start
● making the risks clear (the upsides and the downsides)
● not doing anything without your partner's agreement.

Don't proceed with any plan to change your career without having the people who are important to you fully signed up to the idea. The road ahead will be tough enough without having to deal with the distraction of domestic bickering, particularly when money is tight.

Summary

Many of today's most successful people are those who had the guts and motivation to get out of secure, relatively well-paid jobs and take themselves off in entirely new directions. They took a risk and it paid off.

Today we have been looking at how to view risk correctly in terms of both the upsides and downsides, and how to manage risk as opposed to letting it frighten you. It would be foolish to take a risk just for the sake of it, but putting into effect a well-thought-out plan to change your career and make your life better is an entirely different matter. Having said this, it is only natural to feel hesitant, but this is a good thing because it acts as another check on you to make sure that your dreams are not straying from reality.

Once you have assessed all the risks, don't waver when all the signals are saying 'go'. Seize the moment and – although nobody is pretending what's ahead will be easy or guaranteeing the outcome – don't find yourself years from now regretting that you did nothing.

SUNDAY

MONDAY

TUESDAY

WEDNESDAY

THURSDAY

FRIDAY

SATURDAY

Fact-check (answers at the back)

1. What's the best way to deal with the risk attached to changing career?
   a) Ignore it ❏
   b) Let someone else worry about it ❏
   c) Go on a stress management course ❏
   d) Look at the upsides and downsides and consider both carefully ❏

2. What should you do if your partner is against the idea of you changing career?
   a) Dump him or her ❏
   b) Put the idea on the backburner until you can reach agreement ❏
   c) Ignore your partner's views and carry on regardless ❏
   d) Ask a third party to mediate ❏

3. Which of these will have the greatest impact on your capacity to take risks?
   a) Your domestic circumstances ❏
   b) How much nerve you have ❏
   c) Your track record ❏
   d) How good you are at talking yourself out of tight corners ❏

4. Why is it a good idea to save up some money before you embark on a career change?
   a) So you will have funds to see you through the period at the start when you may have to live on reduced earnings ❏
   b) So you can celebrate by treating yourself to a new car ❏
   c) So you will have some funds if you fail in your new career and end up getting the sack ❏
   d) To make you feel more confident ❏

5. In the context of changing careers, what is 'underfunding'?
   a) Spending too much ❏
   b) Having your application for a loan turned down by the bank ❏
   c) A signal to negotiate a higher salary with your new employer ❏
   d) Not making adequate financial provision for seeing the project through ❏

6. What will you gain by making your finances more flexible?
   a) Fewer money worries ❏
   b) A higher standard of living ❏
   c) More capacity to respond to ups and downs in your earnings ❏
   d) Greater capacity to make savings ❏

7. When is it right to consider short-term borrowings?
   a) When the alternative is not seeing your project through because of lack of funds ❏
   b) When the alternative is doing without a holiday ❏
   c) When you can't face up to living on less ❏
   d) Never: you should not borrow money ❏

8. What's the most important issue to consider when deciding the hours you can work in a part-time job?
   a) Legal limits on working hours ❏
   b) Anything that could come into conflict with your new career ❏
   c) The need to have enough rest ❏
   d) Only doing jobs which are not an insult to your dignity ❏

9. When making a career change, what's good about being in a permanent, stable relationship?
   a) It's a source of moral support ❏
   b) There's nothing good about it (it could hold me back) ❏
   c) Someone else to do the domestic chores ❏
   d) Shared responsibility for paying the bills ❏

10. When is it right to view a change of career as too risky?
   a) When you've got a lot of material possessions and there's too much to lose ❏
   b) When you're over 55 ❏
   c) When the upsides aren't good enough ❏
   d) When you're the family breadwinner ❏

TUESDAY

Mobilizing your talents

Now that you know the direction you're going to go in and what you're seeking to achieve, today you will learn how to turn your dream into reality. Before you start, however, you'll need to make sure that you are ready for this step by asking yourself whether anything is going to get in the way of you realizing your ambitions – is there anything you could put right? You'll also learn how to spot when your plan isn't going as well as it should be and when you may need to step in and take action.

We will be looking at the following topics:

- Do your skills, experience and qualifications match up with what the job market wants or do you fall short in some areas? If you do, what do you need to do about it?
- What systems do you need to put into place to monitor your progress? How are you going to keep a check on whether your project is going to plan or not?
- What paths are open to you and which one are you going to choose?

What do you have to offer?

The next stage in moving your change of career forward is to look at what you have to offer – your bank of skills, experience and qualifications – and to see how it matches up to what a prospective employer would be seeking. The object of this exercise is to determine whether you are ready to launch yourself on to the market, or whether you would improve your chances of making a successful career change by adding to the store of what you have to offer.

Identifying areas of potential disadvantage

Making a career change isn't easy under any circumstances, particularly when it involves selling yourself on the outside job market. This is a subject we will be exploring in full on Thursday. Suffice it to say at this stage that, when seeking a new career, you need as many plus points on your side as possible – and the smallest number of minuses. Let's look at the following case study and see what we can learn from it.

Case study: Megan

Megan wants to branch out into an entirely new career. She has been keeping a careful eye on the job ads in the newspapers and on websites to see what openings there are, the salaries offered and what employers are looking for. What she has gathered so far is that there do seem to be plenty of opportunities and the salaries, while not up to Megan's current level, are still not unreasonable for people starting out at the bottom. Less clear, though, are the qualifications that employers are asking for. In about 80 per cent of cases, the ads mention the examinations of a professional body. Of these, roughly half say that the exams are essential, whereas the rest refer to them as 'desirable' or 'an advantage'.

Megan has also been to see a couple of firms of recruitment consultants and has put to them the question of qualifications. In both cases, they have said that employers show a decided preference for those who have done the professional body's course of study and passed the exams.

The thought of having to enrol at college and do a course of study isn't exactly music to Megan's ears. For a start, she leads a busy life and fitting in attendance at classes with all her other commitments will be challenging, to say the least. There is also the question of course fees to consider; she imagines that they won't come cheap. Most of all, though, she is decidedly unhappy about having to put her plans for a career change on hold for 12 to 18 months while she gets qualified. She sees herself as an achiever and she desperately wants to get on with making a success out of the next part of her life.

Plenty of people in Megan's position would decide to put themselves on the market in unqualified form, even though they know that this will place them at a disadvantage. Like Megan, they want to get on with making their career change as soon as possible, and so they hope that they will come across a sympathetic employer who will see the other qualities they have to offer and give them the opportunity to demonstrate them.

However, people in Megan's position need to give their applications the best possible chance of success by going out into the market with credentials that are as close as they can be to what employers want. In this instance, the feedback is strongly suggesting to Megan that employers want candidates who have passed the professional body's examinations. This, therefore, is what she needs to do.

Deal with any repairable shortfalls in your skills, experience and qualifications before you attempt to put yourself on the market.

Gaining skills and qualifications

Repairing areas of disadvantage, on first inspection, may seem hard. How do you obtain the skills, experience and qualifications you need for your new calling when you're working in a completely different field?

The good news is that access to courses of study has never been better, with providers such as colleges offering something to suit almost everyone's needs. Professional bodies can be particularly helpful when it comes to advising prospective students and you can get information from their websites or by simply ringing them up. Home study courses offer a solution to people who view their circumstances as 'difficult' – for example, people whose jobs call for them to be on the move.

Don't forget that time is on your side when you're considering a visionary career change – time not only to reflect fully on what you're planning to do but also to get the qualifications you need.

Considering the costs

When you are working out how much it is going to cost you to change careers, you should include in your sums not just the monetary effect of having to take a drop in earnings, but also the cost of any courses of study you may have to undertake. The issue of costs figured in Megan's reservations about getting qualified. The first thing to check out is whether any funding exists to help you meet the cost of getting the education and training you need to break into your new career.

Expecting prospective employers to fund the cost of the education and training you need to break into your new career is a mistake. For example, saying to an employer at an interview, 'I'm happy to undertake the course of study for the qualifications I need, providing you fork out the money to pay the bill' isn't going to endear you to them. Not without reason, most employers will view getting the qualifications you need as up to you.

You may strike lucky and find some body or employer who is prepared to fund you, but don't bank on this – particularly when looking at the financial bottom line and the steps you may need to take to make your project viable (the steps we looked at yesterday).

Make sure that you include the cost of education and training in your projections.

Gaining work experience

A factor that has a bearing on how much previous experience you need is the point of entry you are considering for breaking into your new career. Put simply, if you are going in as a trainee, previous experience is not normally a prerequisite. Alternatively, if you are attempting to make the transition a little higher up the ladder, then employers may well be looking for evidence of relevant experience. The driving force in determining your point of entry into a new career is usually money. An absolute beginner won't command such a high salary as someone with relevant job experience.

A further driving force is the fact that having some previous experience will enhance your chances of getting a job. Again, it's what employers want. How do you face up to this one? It may seem impractical to find the time to gain experience in a new area, but it is often possible to do this, as the quotes in the following box illustrate.

Gaining relevant experience

This is what three would-be career changers did to make themselves more employable in their preferred field.

Rosita

'I want to get into hotel and catering management, having spent a lifetime working in local government. To get some experience I got a job working part time in a motel at weekends. Pretty soon I found myself taking bookings, helping the duty manager and sorting out a wide range of administrative problems.'

Carl

'I've worked in retail since leaving school but I've always been interested in IT and I have a long-term ambition to become a systems analyst. Last summer, during my two weeks' holiday, I offered my services for free to a software house based in the local business park. Not only did I get an interesting insight into what went on there, but I also made a lot of useful contacts.'

Siobhan

'I'm a production manager and I work shifts in a food processing and packaging factory. In the fullness of time I want to change direction and go into public relations. To gain experience, when my shifts allow, I work part time with a local firm of media consultants.'

CO-ORDINATION,
AUTHORITY,
LOCAL GEOGRAPHY,
LEADERSHIP...

Stops and checks

Having done all you can to ensure that your skills, experience and qualifications are as close to specification as possible, you now need to put some systems in place that will enable you to check your progress.

The reasons for doing this are threefold:

1 Career aspirations tend to drift over a period of time and since, with a complete change of career, you could be talking about a fairly substantial period, you need to have some way of making sure that you are still on course to achieve what you set out to do originally.
2 The financial plan you put together at the outset was based on certain assumptions, for example the level to which your earnings would reduce and how long it would be before you got back to the level of salary you enjoyed previously. You need to check from time to time that these assumptions are still correct.
3 In the transitional period, you are likely to be heavily dependent on the moral (and perhaps financial) support of those closest to you, for example your partner. Ensuring that you've still got them 'on board' is something you need to do from time to time because, if you haven't, your career-change project could founder.

Draft your career-change proposal

Setting out your career-change plan in writing may sound like going to unnecessary lengths, but there are two good reasons for doing this:

1 It puts on record what you set out to achieve at the beginning and how you saw your plan unfolding (the memory can get hazy on these points).
2 It invests your career-change project with a proper sense of importance.

Firstly, put down a **clear statement of the objective** – for example: 'To move to a career in sales and to be in a sales management position within five years.' This also gives your project a **time period**. This is important, even if at this stage you have little real idea of how long it is going to take you to move from the status of absolute beginner to, say, a junior or middle management position. Factors to take into account are:

● the length of time it might take to find a suitable opening
● the duration of any period of training
● a rough estimate of how long it will take to build up the experience you need to arrive at the objective you have set.

Next comes the **financial part**. Set out any reduction in earnings you predict will arise from your change of career, allowing for the fact that the shortfall will diminish as you gain more experience. Then address the question of how you intend to make up the shortfall: the cash you will need to inject, where it will come from and when – i.e. how often – you will need to draw on it (the subjects we looked at yesterday).

Track the progress of your project

With your plan in writing, you now have a yardstick for measuring how your project is going. Notably, you will be able to tell whether:

● your aims are still the same as they were at the outset
● landing the opening you're seeking is taking an inordinately long time (you may be doing something wrong and perhaps you need to take stock)
● you're overspending – i.e. you need to rethink your finances.

If you find you've not provided enough cash to fund your project properly, take corrective action such as renegotiating your overdraft or working a few extra hours in your part-time job. Making minor adjustments as you go along will help to avoid a headlong plunge into a financial crisis.

Keep your relationships on track

We have stressed the importance of ensuring that those who are nearest and dearest to you share your vision of the future and remain on your side. As career changes move forward, however, what started off as a strong and harmonious partnership can turn sour in the face of harsh reality. For example, the partner in a relationship who's asked to tighten the purse strings or take on a greater share of the financial responsibility may be perfectly happy to begin with but, over a period of time, their commitment could start to waver.

Since the support of the people who are important to you matters as far as the success of your change of career is concerned, you must be attuned to signs of discontent. Include testing the temperature of the water at home in your system of stops and checks.

If you feel the idea of your change of career is starting to wear thin as far as your partner is concerned, take time out to talk it over.

Map your path

What is the best route to follow? Here two options present themselves:

- You can change your career by persuading your employer to give you a chance to do something different.
- Alternatively, you can shop the outside job market for the break you need.

Changing career within organizations

Getting your employer to provide you with the necessary opening to change careers has numerous advantages:

- It is less risky than having to take a step out into the unknown.
- Your current employer will tend to be more supportive, and this support could extend to the provision of training or the payment of course fees, for example.
- With an internal move, you are less likely to have to take a drop in earnings.
- If your career change doesn't work out for any reason, your employer may be able to provide you with a soft landing in the form of a return route back into your old job. (This would not be available with a new employer.)

The difficulty in seeking to make a career change internally is that the opportunity may not be available.

Shopping the outside job market

The disadvantages of having to shop the outside job market for the opening you are seeking mirror in reverse the advantages of going down the internal route:

- It introduces a greater element of risk – at the outset no one knows how they will get on with a new employer.
- A new employer will be less inclined to be supportive over items such as funding the cost of your training.
- They will be less ready to make a special case for you when it comes to pay.
- If you fail in your new career, you may not get very sympathetic treatment – indeed, you shouldn't be too surprised to find yourself out on your ear!

On the other hand, the big advantage of shopping the outside job market is its sheer scale. Unless your ideas are very offbeat, somewhere out there is exactly what you're looking for.

 TIP *Always seek to explore internal opportunities first. Changing careers internally by enlisting the help of your employer is a far less painful route to go along than trying to impress your talents on a potentially suspicious and sometimes unreceptive outside world.*

Summary

Today you have learned what steps you need to take to get your change of career under way. We have looked at whether your chances of getting a job would be enhanced by acquiring more skills, experience and/or qualifications and, if so, how to go about this. We have also examined ways of making sure your project doesn't wander off track either because of lack of commitment or because you got your financial planning wrong.

The path your change of career is going to follow might involve realizing your ambitions internally by making a case to your current employer. Alternatively, you may be deciding to go down the rather more difficult route of accessing opportunities on the open job market.

You are now ready to make a start. You are as prepared as you can be for the challenges you are going to face. What remains is to put the plan into action, which is what we will be looking at over the next few days.

SUNDAY

MONDAY

TUESDAY

WEDNESDAY

THURSDAY

FRIDAY

SATURDAY

Fact-check (answers at the back)

1. What is an area of potential disadvantage?
   a) Having too many big bills to pay ❏
   b) Where your skills/experience/ qualifications fall short of the requirements for your new career ❏
   c) When you don't come from a wealthy background ❏
   d) When you're no good at job interviews ❏

2. What should you do when you don't appear to have the right qualifications to enter the career you've set your sights on?
   a) Find an employer who will sponsor you to do a course ❏
   b) Find an employer who will take you on without the qualifications ❏
   c) Give up and see it as a hopeless cause ❏
   d) See what you can do to get the qualifications ❏

3. Why should you try to get some experience before setting out on your change of career?
   a) You'll get a better appreciation of what the work is really like ❏
   b) You'll stand more chance of getting a job ❏
   c) You'll be able to command a better salary because you won't be going in as a complete beginner ❏
   d) All of the above ❏

4. What should you do when you've got no relevant experience?
   a) See what you can do to get some ❏
   b) Tell employers you've got relevant experience and hope they won't find out ❏
   c) Nothing – it's not your fault ❏
   d) Give up and see it as a hopeless cause ❏

5. Why is it important to keep your financial plan under constant review?
   a) So you know when to ask for a rise ❏
   b) So you know when to call the project off ❏
   c) So you know when you may have to adjust the plan ❏
   d) To impress everyone and show you're in control ❏

6. What should you do if your partner starts to express doubts about the way things are going?
   a) Take no notice ❏
   b) Tell him or her that it's too late to start complaining ❏
   c) Take time out to talk it over ❏
   d) Abandon the project and go back to your old job ❏

7. Why is it always worth seeing if you can make a career change internally?
   a) You won't have to go through the hassle of preparing CVs and writing job applications ❑
   b) It's less risky ❑
   c) You won't have to leave surroundings you've got used to ❑
   d) It will look better on your CV ❑

8. In terms of making a career change, what's good about the outside job market?
   a) Better salaries ❑
   b) You get to meet new people ❑
   c) Its size ❑
   d) It's easier to pull the wool over the eyes of employers who don't know you ❑

9. What could be the biggest stumbling block when trying to effect a career change internally?
   a) The opportunities may not be available ❑
   b) Your boss ❑
   c) Office politics ❑
   d) No one will take you seriously ❑

10. What do you say to employers who are prepared to offer you the start you want in a new career but who will only pay you a beginner's wage?
    a) See if you can negotiate a higher rate ❑
    b) Turn the offer down ❑
    c) Turn them down and post your views on the employer's pay scales on a social networking website ❑
    d) Accept the offer as it stands and thank them for the opportunity ❑

WEDNESDAY

Realizing career changes internally

The internal path towards making a career change is one that many people mistakenly ignore. They pitch themselves straight on to the outside job market and don't think to explore what could be available to them through a far simpler and less hazardous method. Getting your current employer to provide you with the opportunity you are seeking is a decidedly less painful route than stepping into a new job with an unknown new employer.

Today we will look at:

- profiling organizations – analysing which employers would be likely to back you and which wouldn't
- assessing your value to your employer – what will make your employer say yes
- making your pitch – how to make a case
- monitoring your progress
- contingency plans – catering for career changes that go wrong, and having an escape route available.

Why internal career changes are easier

First, let's remind ourselves again why it is easier to switch careers by moving around within organizations than it is to find a new employer to underwrite our ideas. Some of these points are ones we touched on yesterday:

- There is less risk in staying with the same employer. While the outside job market may have a greater range of opportunities, joining a new employer is still largely a step into the unknown.
- Similarly, if your change of career doesn't go to plan for any reason, an employer who has known you for some time will be more inclined to provide you with an escape route – usually in the form of a U-turn back to the job you did previously.
- If your current employer is backing your change of career, their support is more likely to extend to the provision of training.
- Questions like salary (and any need for it to be reduced) will be handled more sensitively. You may even find that your employer is prepared to maintain your earnings at their current level.
- You'll have a lot more sway over an employer who knows your track record. As a consequence, they are far more likely to accede to any requests you make.

Profiling your organization

Profiling your organization is a way of determining whether it is capable of delivering the opportunity you are seeking. Ask yourself some questions under the following headings:

Structure
If, for example, you want to get into R & D, does your organization have an R & D department?

Culture
Organizations vary greatly in their 'people-mindedness'. Some go to great lengths to retain staff and accommodate ambitions, whereas others don't. What is the prevailing ethos in your organization?

Performance

Organizations that are performing well will be more inclined to invest in people. How is your organization doing against accepted measures such as profitability and market share.

Personalities

Key figures such as your boss will have a big say in how the organization receives your case for changing careers. Can you count on their backing or not?

The art of the possible

Profiling is not about making value judgements, such as whether you work for a good firm or a bad one, but about forming an objective view of your organization's capability of delivering the opportunity you are seeking. You may, for example, work for an extremely nice bunch of people who take great pains to look after you and everyone else but this won't do you much good if the opportunity you're seeking simply isn't there.

However, the art of the possible is about seeing what is there and using it to your advantage. Organizations won't always bend to your aspirations, but they have needs and identifying these needs can work in your favour. If your organization values you, they can sometimes be persuaded to create something for you that did not previously exist.

TIP *Don't write off your organization simply because what's there at the moment doesn't appear to match your aspirations. There's always the possibility that you can use your leverage to get them to create an opportunity for you.*

Be flexible

The following case study illustrates the importance of flexibility. You should never put up barriers to changing your mind in the light of (a) experience and (b) the existence of real opportunities. Many career-change success stories centre on cases of people who have gone with the flow and taken advantage of opportunities that are there. This contrasts with those who continue year after year in pursuit of hard-to-achieve or impossible goals.

Assessing your leverage

The capacity of your organization to provide you with the opportunity you are seeking is one half of the equation. The other half is you. Not to put too fine a point on it, what do you have in your favour that will persuade your employer to give your ideas a sympathetic ear?

Ultimately, your employer's willingness to give you a chance will depend on the value they place on you. Do they see you as someone they want to retain in the organization – someone they wouldn't want to say no to in case you decided to leave?

Your job performance obviously plays a great part in determining how far your employer will be prepared to go to accommodate your ambitions. If you've been a consistently high performer, your employer would probably be sad to lose you. After all, good people are scarce. On the other hand, if your performance has been mediocre, don't expect too much effort to go into providing you with opportunities. The same goes for conduct. If your track record is squeaky clean, you'll attract more favourable treatment than if you have accumulated a collection of black marks against your name.

The following factors will also have a bearing on your worth to your employer:

● You have a lot of know-how about your organization and the way it operates – know-how that, for example, would be useful to a competitor.
● You are seen as a key member of the team. Your contribution to the team's efforts would be missed and hard to replace.
● You possess scarce skills on which your employer relies.

Considerations such as these will help you form a view of how receptive your employer is going to be to any case you put forward.

When your value to your employer is low

What if you don't score heavily on any of these counts? What if, for example, your job performance hasn't been up to scratch recently? Where does this place you in terms of having the necessary authority to make your employer sit up and listen when you put forward your case?

Needless to say, warning signals should be flashing at you by this point – warning signals telling you that you shouldn't be building up too many hopes. But before you finally abandon the internal path to realizing your ambitions, bear in mind that you can *acquire* value to your employer. For example, if your work has been slipshod, you can mend your ways. If your skills are lacking, you can take steps to polish them up. In short, the time may not be right just yet but six months down the line – and with a little concerted effort – who knows?

Your silent bargaining power

It is worth dwelling on this term for a few moments because it sums up the nature of the leverage you are hoping to bring to bear on your employer. To achieve anything – whether you are going for a promotion, trying to get a pay rise or, as in this case, trying to branch out into a different field – you need silent bargaining power on your side. Why is it 'silent'?

Once you think about it, you'll realize that the message you are delivering is a subtle one. You are stating your aims and at the same time making it clear that you are determined to achieve your aims. This is a way of telling your employer – without spelling it out – that, if they turn you down, they run the risk of you taking your talents elsewhere. Employers won't be slow to grasp the point but, importantly, you've not said anything that could be taken as a threat. Threats, as we will be seeing shortly, are not good because they invite negative responses. The threat is *implied* rather than put into words.

Making your pitch

We have now arrived at the point where you have satisfied yourself that:

- your employer is capable of providing you with the opportunity you are seeking
- you have enough leverage to make them sit up and listen.

The next step is deciding how you're going to present your case.

Who to speak to

It hardly needs saying, but the first person you should speak to is your immediate boss. This is for the simple reason that your boss is going to be a key figure in realizing your ambitions. You will do much better if you have your boss on your side.

- Your boss is in a better position than you when it comes to making internal job moves happen and which strings to pull.
- Your silent bargaining power will be at its most effective when used on your boss.
- Globally speaking, your boss probably has more experience than you and may be able to give you advice, including points you haven't considered before.

With your boss on your side, you will stand a far better chance of being able to return to your old job if, for some reason, the change of career doesn't work out.

What to say

Even if your boss is the first to hear about your ideas on the path you now want your career to take, there is still plenty of scope for the message to come across badly. Your boss might think you are dissatisfied or have a criticism about the way you are being managed. However, there are ways to avoid this.

Be positive.

First of all, make sure that everything you say is positive. Don't, for example, say that you're bored or that you can't see any prospects with the job you're doing now – even if it's true. Instead, make a point of saying what you've gained from the experience, how much you've enjoyed working with your colleagues and the skills you've acquired. As to your ideas on where you see your career going next, put these in the context of wishing to remain with the organization, hence the reason for seeking to make the move internally.

Don't make threats.

It's tempting at moments like this to round off what you're saying by spelling out what you would do if you're not given the opportunity you're seeking, i.e. go off and try your chances elsewhere. This approach would be a mistake. No matter how carefully you couch your words, it will be taken as a threat and threats, unfortunately, don't always get the results we want. In this case, your boss could take you at your word and tell you that, if you're so confident, perhaps you should go and try to sell your talents elsewhere. This then leaves you with the problem of what to do now. At this stage, you probably won't have given too much thought to the idea of leaving. So do you put up (go out on the job market when you're not really ready) or shut up (stay put and lose a big slice of your credibility)?

TIP *Remember the fundamental point about silent bargaining power: the threat is implied rather than put into words.*

Maintain credibility.

Credibility, already mentioned, is important because, if silent bargaining power is going to work for you, your boss has got to believe you're serious about what you're saying. Making threats you can't (or don't want to) carry out is one way of putting a dent in your credibility.

Monitoring your progress

What you are hoping for is that your silent bargaining power works and you get the boss's backing. If you do, the potential benefits for you are considerable:

- The boss could put out feelers for you and speak to the right people.
- The boss could keep his or her ear to the ground.
- At the appropriate moment, the boss could say the right things about you.
- The boss could make your ambitions known to higher management.
- The boss could come to your rescue if the career change goes wrong.
- A boss who is on your side would not be doing anything to put a spoke in your wheel.

However, what if nothing happens? What if months go by and the subject of your change of career is never mentioned again?

Give your employer a time limit

Even in the most people-friendly organizations, it would be wrong to expect doors to be opened for you overnight. On the other hand, it would be equally wrong to allow long periods of time to go by with nothing tangible to show, because it could mean one of two things:

- Your silent bargaining power didn't work – you thought you had some leverage but you got it wrong.
- The opportunities you're looking for come up only occasionally so, in real terms, what you're seeking to do isn't realizable.

In both cases, this is a signal to you to turn your attention to the outside job market. The fact that you're doing this is, of course, something you can keep to yourself so, if your employer is still trying to come up with an opening for you, they will keep trying. In effect, you will then have two sets of irons in the fire – internal and external – at the same time.

Creating your own role

You can use your silent bargaining power in another way to exert leverage on your employer. Many people have been successful in using their silent bargaining power to create special roles for themselves. Lorna, in the following case study, is an example of this. She has the same human resources management ambitions as Della, whose case we looked at earlier.

Case study: Lorna

Lorna works in sales for a company that employs around 200 people and has plans for major expansion over the next two years. Lorna wants to get into human resources management and, with this aim in mind, she has been getting the appropriate professional qualifications by studying in her own time. However, her company doesn't have a human resources department. The function is performed by a combination of muddling along and, for recruitment, paying employment agencies to provide staff.

Lorna started looking for a job in human resources management six months ago. She has applied for a number of positions but only once got as far as an interview. Her problem, she quickly found, is lack of experience. Most of the jobs she has applied for stipulate that candidates should ideally have two or three years' experience. To Lorna this is all very frustrating. How is she supposed to get the experience if no one is prepared to give her a chance?

One day Lorna happens to catch sight of an invoice from an employment agency and it gives her an idea. The invoice is for the recruitment of a new staff member and it is for what seems like a large sum of money. Later on, she does some calculations. Using an estimate of the staff turnover of the business, she works out roughly what the company must be spending on agencies' fees and the figure she comes up with shocks her.

For a fraction of what the company is paying, she reckons she could provide an in-house human resources function that would take in everything, including recruitment. The savings on agencies' bills alone would be enormous, bearing in mind the need for additional staff that the expansion plan will entail.

Lorna first tries bouncing her ideas off her boss, Mike. Initially, Mike doesn't seem very interested, until he realizes that Lorna isn't going to go away without an answer from him. What also starts to play on Mike's mind is that, if Lorna doesn't get her way, she might choose to try her luck elsewhere. What bothers him most is the thought of Lorna joining one of the company's competitors and taking important customers with her. Finally, Mike agrees to have a word with Gemma, the CEO.

Gemma listens carefully to what Mike has to say. She knows that Lorna does a good job in sales, so she takes the point straight away that it would be a mistake to force her into the arms of a competitor. As to the idea of Lorna setting up a one-woman human resources function, Gemma is impressed by the case she puts forward, notably the savings in agency fees. She decides to let Lorna give it a go for six months, explaining that it is up to Lorna to prove that an in-house human resources function can contribute to the business and not be just another add-on cost.

Points to pick out from Lorna's case study are as follows:

● Lorna has a lot of silent bargaining power, thanks to her position in sales and the high regard in which she is held.
● Getting Mike on her side is critical. Although Mike doesn't have the authority to sanction a new HR department, he is able to use his influence with Gemma (who does).
● Putting up a case based on cost savings is a good move. Illustrating the benefits for the company adds another convincing reason for giving Lorna a chance.

Contingency plans

As a rule, we don't go into career changes contemplating failure. Rather, we feel confident of our ability to put our talents to use in a different field. The only outcome we consider, therefore, is our success and this is why having a contingency plan up our sleeve doesn't always occur to us.

There is also another problem here. When you are locked in a negotiation with your employer, you may think that it won't sound very good if you start raising questions about what happens if you fail. You end up, therefore, not saying anything.

Nevertheless, it's important to consider all the possible outcomes, including negative ones. If you don't address all the potential outcomes, you could find yourself several months down the track with nowhere to go if the new career turns out to be a big mistake. As we said at the start of today's chapter, making the switch into a new career internally has big advantages, one of which is the far greater chance of an escape route being provided for you if the move doesn't go to plan. However, even in this situation the way back into your old job may not be available because someone has already been taken on to replace you.

Bear in mind, too, that there are other reasons why it's sensible to have an escape route open. For example, the slot that's been created for you could come under scrutiny as part of some future headcount slashing exercise. You're the one with least experience, so unexpectedly your shift into a new career culminates not in greater job fulfilment but in you finding yourself at the top of a redundancy list.

Negotiate trial terms

Negotiating trial terms is all well and good if, as in Lorna's case, the idea comes from your employer. But what if it doesn't? What if nothing is said about the terms of your transfer? This is where you are left with having to raise the matter yourself. It may be difficult to do this without it looking as if you don't have total confidence in your ability.

The answer is to turn the tables, by which we mean pointing out to your employer the benefits for them in making everything conditional on the outcome of a trial. If it doesn't work out, you could say that you would be quite happy to go back to your old job, and what could be more reasonable than that? The last thing you want is to be a problem to them.

Get it in writing

Some employers will, as a matter of course, provide you with details of your new appointment in writing – including confirmation of the trial period and the availability of your old job for a defined period. Some employers may, however, require a little prompting.

Is it worth pushing to get your trial terms set out in writing? We would say yes – largely so that there are no misunderstandings and everyone is clear about what has been agreed.

Summary

Today we looked at the advantages of realizing career-change ambitions internally, assuming that a path is available. We have seen how it pays to check out the option of internal transfer first before launching yourself on to the turbid waters of the open job market – discussed tomorrow.

We have also seen how you have a potentially powerful weapon in the shape of silent bargaining power, which you can use to exert leverage. You can even use this leverage to persuade an organization to create a new role – a niche just for you. You also learned about the importance of keeping tabs on your employer so that you're not left hanging on with half-promises.

Finally, even if the use of silent bargaining power does pay off, don't overlook the need to provide yourself with escape routes. Of these, by far the most practical is to have some way back into your old job. This may not be the most satisfactory outcome but it will give you a safe haven from where you can take stock before setting off again.

SUNDAY
MONDAY
TUESDAY
WEDNESDAY
THURSDAY
FRIDAY
SATURDAY

Fact-check (answers at the back)

1. In the context of what we have done today, what's the purpose of profiling?
   a) To see where your organization stands in terms of its ability to provide you with opportunities ❏
   b) A point-scoring exercise to see how your employer compares with others ❏
   c) To rate how your employer performs when it comes to dealing with people issues ❏
   d) A way of gathering evidence to make a case for changing your career ❏

2. What is the art of the possible?
   a) Seeing everything in a positive light ❏
   b) Taking advantage of opportunities that are there ❏
   c) Focusing on what you can do rather than what you can't ❏
   d) Emancipation from a dead-end job ❏

3. What is silent bargaining power?
   a) Leverage you can use on your employer, based on your worth to them ❏
   b) Threats you can make to your employer if you don't get what you want ❏
   c) Power based on body language rather than speech ❏
   d) Bargaining power that has no impact ❏

4. What carries the most influence when it comes to getting your employer to agree to a career change?
   a) Threatening to resign if you don't get what you want ❏
   b) Threatening to raise a grievance ❏
   c) Your silent bargaining power ❏
   d) Offering to work for a reduced salary ❏

5. Who should you speak to first about your wish to move into a different field of work?
   a) The human resources manager ❏
   b) Your boss ❏
   c) The manager of the team you want to join ❏
   d) The CEO ❏

6. After three months in a new role, your employer tells you that the position they created for you can no longer be sustained but, as an alternative to redundancy, they offer you a job in the line of work you did previously. How should you respond?
   a) Ask to be made redundant then take your chance on the outside job market ❏
   b) Raise a grievance on the grounds that you've not been given a fair chance ❏
   c) Accept the position ❏
   d) Accept, but at the same time start looking round at what other employers can offer ❏

7. Which of these is the best argument to put forward to an employer for bringing in house a function that is currently outsourced?
a) It will create a slot for you ❑
b) You'll do a better job than the outside service provider ❑
c) It will save money ❑
d) You'll leave if they don't ❑

8. Your employer has agreed to give you a try in a field of work completely new to you. How much should they pay you?
a) The same as your current salary ❑
b) The rate for the job ❑
c) (a) then (b) after a trial period ❑
d) Whatever they decide ❑

9. What do we mean by an escape route?
a) A way out if the plan to break into a new career goes wrong ❑
b) Finding the opportunity you want with a new employer ❑
c) Another term for a golden handshake ❑
d) Part of the fire drill ❑

10. When you broach the subject of making a career change, your boss is non-committal and won't be drawn. What should you do?
a) See it as a bad sign and start sending off job applications ❑
b) Have another go at presenting a case, more forcefully this time ❑
c) Wait and see whether your silent bargaining power starts to work ❑
d) Go over your boss's head and speak to someone higher up the ladder ❑

THURSDAY

Attacking the outside job market

We've arrived at the point where we've exhausted the internal route to realizing our ambition to change our career. Now we must look to the outside world to provide us with the opportunity we are seeking.

Today we will cover:

- assessing the task – how employers see people like you, and what it takes to convince prospective employers that you're serious
- how to pitch yourself at the outside job market – designing a cover letter and CV that will work for you and the messages you need to get across
- preparing yourself for the hard knocks – how to view rejection and how to evaluate success; the importance of 'keeping going'
- exploring the invisible job market – using proactive sourcing methods to find out about jobs that aren't advertised and why the invisible market may have more to offer
- networking as a way of accessing opportunities – using your contacts to open doors for you.

Assessing the task

Shopping the outside job market is an entirely different matter from accessing career-change opportunities internally. It has some disadvantages, as follows:

- You don't have the advantage of dealing with people you know. As a consequence, silent bargaining power won't help you.
- Competition is a factor – you won't be the only one with your eyes on the opportunities.
- Because of the difficulties, there is an ever-present danger of discouragement (giving up prematurely because you feel you can't take any more).
- Changing employers is inherently risky.
- There is a greater likelihood of you having to take a drop in earnings.
- The U-turns won't be available to you. In fact, if you fail in your new career, there is every possibility that you will be shown the door.

However, what the job market does have going for it is its size.

How employers see it

First, let's try to appreciate how an employer would see someone like you who comes out of the blue with all sorts of grand ideas about making a fresh start in life. Are you in need of therapy, perhaps? Or temporarily out of touch with reality? In short, there is a credibility gap straight away. Are you serious? Have you thought through the money implications properly?

The trouble is that employers aren't green in these matters. They've taken people on trust before, only to find that their trust was misplaced and the people became thorns in their side.

Bridging the credibility gap

Becoming aware of employers' concerns will help you highlight some of the obstacles you need to overcome in order to convince them that you deserve to be given a chance. You need to persuade a potential employer that:

● you are serious and that this is an idea you have researched properly, and not just something you have dreamed up overnight
● you have thought through the ramifications of living on a lower (starter's) salary
● you have gone one step further and planned your finances for the foreseeable future to take account of reduced earnings.

Pitching yourself at the market

To an outsider, the job market can seem a bewildering place. Here it helps to view it as two separate markets that you tap into in quite different ways:

1 **The visible market**
   These are the jobs you see advertised in the press or on websites. They are there for everyone to see. It is simply a question of keeping your eyes open.
2 **The invisible market**
   This is the unadvertised sector – the jobs employers keep to themselves for a variety of reasons.

Reactive and proactive sourcing

Reactive and proactive sourcing are simply terms to describe the different methods you use to access these two markets:

- **Reactive sourcing** is aimed at the visible market, where the employer provides the stimulus in the form of advertising. The quality of the response you make to this stimulus is what counts.
- **Proactive sourcing** is where you provide the stimulus. Proactive sourcing is designed to penetrate the invisible market.

Don't miss out on the invisible market by confining your job hunting to scanning ads. Give some thought, instead, to making a greater use of proactive methods to source the opportunities you are looking for.

Designing an effective cover letter and CV

This is where you start. Before you go out on the external job market you need to give some thought to what you are going to say about yourself and, in particular, what you are going to say to employers who may be sceptical about your seriousness and commitment. The place to do this is in your CV and in the cover letter you design to go with it.

Cover letters

Cover letters are important because they are what employers read first. Your cover letter is therefore an ideal place to tell employers that you are serious about changing careers and that you have given a great deal of thought to how you're going to do it. The following box shows an example of what a candidate had to say about himself in a cover letter we received:

My ambition is to move into _____ and to make a complete change of career. My reasons are as follows:

- I feel my _____ skills would be put to better use and that this would be beneficial both to myself and to any future employer.
- I have taken courses of home study as detailed in my CV and I feel this now qualifies me to apply for my first position.
- I believe I could be highly successful in _____ and enjoy much better prospects.
- I realize that I would have to start at the bottom of the ladder and that there could be financial implications in the short term. Fortunately, my wife is in a position to work additional hours and, in this way, we should be able to make up any shortfall.

This statement is good in the following respects:

- It's **clear and concise** – no one is left in any doubt that this is someone seeking a change of career as opposed to someone who's replied to the wrong ad or whose motives aren't clear.
- It's **positive** – the candidate doesn't air any gripes about his present career.
- It identifies the candidate's **transferable talents**.
- The mention of the home-study courses highlights the candidate's **commitment** to his idea.
- The reference to his wife's capacity to take on extra work pre-empts one of employers' principal concerns about people who are seeking to change careers – namely that they haven't thought through the **financial implications** properly.

CVs

The same message about changing careers has got to come across in your CV. You need to convey not only the fact that you are planning a career change but also the fact that you have skills that are relevant to the new career.

- **Focus on your ambition**

  The best place to do this is in a section headed 'Aims' or 'Ambitions', which you should put on the front page of your CV, right after your personal information. The reason for this advice is that the fact you're trying to change your career is pivotal to any reading of what follows. It is quite easy in these situations for employers to misread your intentions or to think there's been a mix-up and you've applied for the wrong job.

- **Keep it relevant**

  Most of you will know already the importance of keeping information in your cover letters and CVs relevant to the job for which you're applying. In normal circumstances what you've done in previous jobs will be relevant, but this is where applications aimed at making a change of career are different. What you've done before won't for the most part have any bearing on what you're seeking to do now, so don't go into reams of detail on your past employment history. By all means present an overview to show you've built up a good track record in your current line of work but, at the same time, bring into play:

  - your transferable talents
  - details of any relevant work experience and training you have done (including self-study).

In interviews, expect employers to probe you on their concerns and stand by for tough questions. Your aim in handling these questions is to keep the messages consistent with the messages in your cover letter and CV.

Preparing for the hard knocks

You can strike lucky but, on the whole, the job market can be an inhospitable place for people who want to change their careers. Discouragement is one of the unfortunate spin-offs of using the external job market to achieve an aim that is intrinsically difficult.

The market has a decided preference for candidates who can offer previous experience. Not only will training times be reduced, but there is less risk with a candidate who has done the job before. As a result, if you are a candidate who can offer no experience, you may just get the brush-off, usually in the form of a standard 'sorry, but no thank you' letter. You aren't given the reasons for your rejection and your overall impression is that you are banging your head against a brick wall. It's small wonder, therefore, that you feel you are in a catch-22 situation – you can't get the job because you haven't got the experience and you haven't got the experience because you can't get the job.

What we are seeing is one of the hazards of attacking the visible or advertised market. By its very nature it is highly competitive and among the competition there is bound to be someone (or several people) with experience. Put more of your effort into the invisible market, where competition is less of a problem.

Keep your expectations realistic when you're shopping the visible market. See rejections as the norm and learn to live with them. Keep in mind that this is not the same as trying to find a job in a field where you have got experience.

When job prospecting, we tend to categorize success and failure in terms of:

- the number of interviews we get
- how many interviews turn into jobs.

With career changes, however, the rules are different. Success is our capacity to keep going against what can sometimes seem like insurmountable odds. Failure is giving up.

Accessing the 'invisible market'

Most vacancies aren't filled as a result of advertising. Instead, employers use a range of alternative recruitment methods which, collectively, make up the invisible market. Among these methods are:

- **recruitment agencies**
  Employers recruit staff by asking agencies (recruitment consultants) to search their files for suitable candidates.
- **files of previous applicants**
  Employers look back though their files of previous applicants. This includes people who have sent in unsolicited CVs.

Competition is rarely a factor on the invisible market. Indeed, it is not unusual to find that you are the only applicant – it's a one-horse race. By contrast, the visible market is a place where competition, in the shape of other, more experienced applicants, presents a tough challenge for people looking for opportunities to change their career.

Systematic cold-calling

Phoning up selected employers to see if they have anything suitable for you is one easy proactive method of accessing the invisible market. However, cold-calling an organization just once and leaving your name, address and telephone contact numbers is pretty pointless, for the following reasons:

- One cold call reveals only a single snapshot of an organization at a particular point in time.

● When an opportunity does come up, it's a safe bet that the piece of paper with your name on it will have disappeared.

Here's the proper way to go about cold-calling:

1 **Identify the right organizations.**
For career changers, this means the kind of organizations that are likely to have career-start jobs in their chosen field. Find out which organizations these are by talking to friends and other contacts, and by keeping your eyes on the newspapers and websites to see who's advertising for people in the line of work that interests you.

2 **Speak to the right person.**
This means getting hold of the decision maker. For example, if you're trying to access a career in logistics, the person you need to speak to is the logistics manager. To find out his or her name, simply ring up and ask.

3 **Keep the call brief.**
Remember that cold calls have the potential to be annoying, so explain quickly who you are, where you're coming from and what you're seeking to achieve. Ask if there's anything suitable for you at the moment. If the answer's yes, ask them what to do next. If the answer's no, thank them for their time in such a way that will enable you to ring again another time.

4 **Keep a record of your calls.**
Jot down the name of the person you spoke to, the date and any interesting information you picked up.

5 **Work out a call cycle.**
Score your calls on a scale of 0–5. Your 5s are employers who are worth keeping in touch with regularly. At the other extreme, zero any no-hopers or employers who give you a hard time. From these scores, you will be able to work out a call cycle: identify organizations that are worth ringing every three months or so against those that may warrant a call only occasionally. Be ready to amend your scorings.

TIP *The knack to cold-calling is to keep doing it. Keep getting those snapshots and you'll eventually build a detailed picture of your target organizations.*

Systematic cold-calling carried out in this way eventually yields results. You will find yourself making fewer and fewer calls, but the calls will become increasingly targeted. Statistical probability takes over from pure chance, and sooner or later you will start to connect with good opportunities.

Mailshots

Another way of accessing the invisible market is to send a copy of your CV as a mailshot to selected employers, to see what opportunities they have. Here, again, is the right way to go about it:

1 **Identify the right organizations.**
   As with cold calls, identify organizations that are likely to have the kind of opportunities you are looking for.
2 **Phone first.**
   Again, find out the name of the right person to send it to.
3 **Compose a cover letter**.
   Keep this short and use it to reiterate the main messages in your CV – where you're coming from, what you're seeking to achieve and evidence that you are serious.
4 **Mark your envelope 'Confidential'.**
   This is the best way of ensuring that the right person opens it.

The aim with a mailshot is either to connect with an opportunity or, if one isn't immediately available, to get your CV filed in a place where it will be revisited when an opportunity next comes up.

Agencies

Getting your name on the files of the right agencies – also called recruitment consultants – is another excellent way to access the invisible market. Good agencies will be able to use their know-how and contacts to help you access the right kind of opportunities. As such, they are another useful point of entry into the invisible market where competition isn't a major issue.

Here is the right way to go about it:

1 **Pick the right ones.**
  To be any use to you, the agencies you choose have to deal with appointments in the field you are trying to get into.
2 **Make sure they understand you.**
  Take great pains to explain to agencies that you are seeking to make a *change of career*. This is to stop them hounding you with vacancies in the field in which you currently work, i.e. the field you are trying to leave. It will be much easier for an agency to find you a job in a line of work where you have experience and, because agencies are results-oriented (the normal arrangement is for the fees they charge to become payable only when someone starts in a job), there is a real danger of this happening.
3 **Keep in contact.**
  Ring up your chosen agencies from time to time, especially if you have heard nothing from them. Not only will it remind them that you are still there but you might pick up some interesting feedback on why they are having no joy finding the kind of opportunity you are looking for. Is it because what you are seeking to do is unrealistic – which might be a cue to take stock – or because the agency is useless?

Professional networking

Professional networking is by far the best way of accessing career-change opportunities. The following case study is an example of how it can work:

Case study: Rachel

Rachel is a buyer for a large sportswear retailer. For some years, she has been nurturing an ambition to get out of retail and try her hand at gymnasium and fitness centre management. Clearly, some of the knowledge she has picked up in the sportswear trade is transferable to her new career, but Rachel realizes that, wherever she goes, she is going to have to start at the bottom.

For the last 18 months, Rachel has been applying for practically every post she has seen advertised. So far, however, the results have been disappointing. At her only interview, the interviewer told her that he thought she was making a mistake by trying to change her career. More recently, Rachel has tried sending her CV to a list of selected employers. Again, the results have been disappointing. Some wrote back to say they would keep her details on file, but most simply ignored her.

One of Rachel's contacts is Tim, who used to be an accountant in Rachel's company. He moved on two years ago and is now financial controller for a group of companies with interests in the hotel and leisure industry. Rachel has always kept in touch with Tim and they meet occasionally, either for lunch or for a game of squash. At one of these meetings, Rachel mentions the applications she is making and asks Tim if he has any contacts in the fitness industry. Tim says that, strangely enough, his company has just acquired a business with a small chain of fitness centres and he would be happy to have a word with the person who runs them.

Two days later, Tim calls Rachel to say that he has spoken to the manager of the fitness centres who is very interested to hear about Rachel because she has been intending to recruit an assistant for some time. It's now left to Rachel to ring up this person and arrange an interview.

The case study shows that Rachel's attack on the visible market didn't have much success, which is fairly typical. However, talking to her former colleague yielded a much better result: an interview in which she stands a reasonable chance of getting the job.

This case study demonstrates the power of networking in the following ways:

- Networking can access the invisible market – in this instance, a job that hasn't been advertised yet. Put another way, this is a case of getting in before the competition arrives.
- The fact that the manager of the fitness centres knew Tim and that Tim knew Rachel helped put any doubts about Rachel's character to rest.
- By giving Rachel a job, the manager of the fitness centres will be doing Tim a favour. Some day the manager of the fitness centres may want a favour from Tim in return. In other words, there is an element of self-interest at work – a reminder that 'I'll scratch your back if you scratch mine' is a fundamental part of networking.

For the magic to work, the person you're networking with has got to hold you in sufficiently high regard to want to stick his or her neck out for you. Presumably, Tim held Rachel in high regard; otherwise, he would not have put her name forward.

The lifelong interview

Paying attention to the image you project to your professional colleagues is what we refer to as the 'lifelong interview' and it is a critical part of successful networking. It means, for example, applying some of the gloss you normally save up for job interviews to every day. You are on your best behaviour – always. You give your work your best shot and, most importantly, you learn to keep your flaws to yourself.

It is interesting to speculate on how Tim would have reacted to Rachel's enquiry if he had not held her in such high esteem. Would he have kept his mouth shut about the newly acquired business with its chain of fitness centres and told Rachel that he couldn't help?

The case study underlines the fact that, for professional networking to work for you, your contacts have got to want to be associated with you. They won't, for example, feel this way if they know of any blots on your record, if you're unreliable or your work is poor. They'll keep their distance, and who would blame them? At the end of the day, it's their own reputation that they're putting on the line.

It's not easy to put the lifelong interview into practice. The consistency and application called for are difficult to achieve.

Summary

Today we looked at what you can gain from shopping the job market, along with some of the problems. On the plus side, the sheer size of the market and its diversity mean that, providing you're realistic, someone out there somewhere will be prepared to offer you the opportunity you are seeking. You learned how to connect with these opportunities and how to pitch yourself at the market correctly. You need to identify yourself as someone who's serious about wanting to change careers and who's thought through the ramifications.

We stressed the importance of designing a cover letter and CV that pre-empt the concerns employers have about people who are taking an apparently backward step. You will only overcome the barriers in employers' minds by addressing them and engaging with them – not by leaving employers to form their own opinions.

We also looked at the problems you'll face when you start to make applications, particularly the problem of competition from people with more experience. Finally, you learned the importance of making sure that you don't overlook the invisible market, where competition isn't such a big issue.

SUNDAY

MONDAY

TUESDAY

WEDNESDAY

THURSDAY

FRIDAY

SATURDAY

Fact-check (answers at the back)

1. What is the danger of discouragement?
   a) The feeling of being undervalued ❏
   b) Drowning your sorrows in alcohol ❏
   c) Sleepless nights ❏
   d) Giving up because you feel you can't take any more ❏

2. What is the best way of convincing employers you're serious about changing your career?
   a) Talking confidently when you go for interviews ❏
   b) Showing to them you've researched your ideas properly and thought through the financial implications ❏
   c) Telling them what's wrong with the career you're in now and why you want to leave it ❏
   d) Offering to work for nothing ❏

3. What is the biggest difficulty you face when applying for jobs on the invisible market?
   a) The cost attached to making phone calls and sending out mailshots ❏
   b) Employers who don't reply ❏
   c) Connecting with suitable vacancies ❏
   d) The whole exercise could be a waste of time ❏

4. What is the biggest difficulty you face when applying for jobs on the visible market?
   a) Competition from applicants with more experience ❏
   b) Finding out about suitable vacancies ❏
   c) Having to write cover letters and CVs ❏
   d) Going for interviews that are time-wasters ❏

5. What is proactive sourcing?
   a) Sourcing aimed at accessing the visible market ❏
   b) Sourcing aimed at accessing the invisible market ❏
   c) Sourcing aimed at accessing both markets ❏
   d) Sourcing highly paid jobs ❏

6. When changing careers, how do you measure success when you're applying for jobs on the visible market?
   a) By the number of applications you send off ❏
   b) By the number of interviews you get ❏
   c) By how long you can keep going ❏
   d) By how many employers reply to you ❏

7. What's the aim of cold-calling employers?
a) To introduce yourself to them ❏
b) As (a) but to ask them at the same time to keep you in mind for any opportunities which might come up ❏
c) There is no point – it's a waste of time ❏
d) To give a snapshot of what's available at the time ❏

8. What works best when accessing career-change opportunities on the outside job market?
a) Reactive sourcing ❏
b) Proactive sourcing ❏
c) Registering with agencies ❏
d) Professional networking ❏

9. What is the 'lifelong interview'?
a) Projecting the right image and doing it every day ❏
b) Using every opportunity to learn something new ❏
c) An interview for a high-profile job ❏
d) An interview where they ask questions about your childhood ❏

10. When accessing career-change opportunities by professional networking, which of these will weigh most in your favour?
a) Your ability to win friends and influence people ❏
b) How much socializing you do ❏
c) Your lifelong interview ❏
d) The number of people you know ❏

FRIDAY

Facing a forced career change

Throughout this week we've made the distinction between visionary career changes, inspired by the wish for something better, and those forced on us by events outside our control. At some point in your life you may discover that you have to find another way of making a living and that you have no choice in the matter. This might be because of changed personal circumstances such as a medical condition or – increasingly likely these days – because your career has vanished as a result of advances in technology or a shift in global markets.

Today we focus our attention on these no-choice situations. The topics we'll cover are as follows:

- compressing your project into a short timescale because the clock is ticking against you and you need results quickly
- multiple targeting – improving your chances of success by pursuing more than one aim at a time
- stopgap measures: what to do when you run out of time
- the Trojan Horse technique – using the market for short-term or temporary work to open doors that would otherwise stay closed.

The need for quick results

With visionary career changes, you can afford to take as long as you like to see your project through. By contrast, when your change of career has been dictated by external events, time is against you.

How long have you got?

Putting a timescale on how long you've got helps to sharpen your thinking. Do as follows:

- If you're facing redundancy, you may already have been given a finishing date. If you haven't, it would be reasonable to ask for one or at least to be given a rough idea.
- If a medical condition is the reason for having to change career, talk it over with your doctor and get an opinion on how quickly you need to act.
- If your career change is driven by other personal circumstances, see whether you can put in place any interim arrangements that would give you breathing space. For example, if you are now responsible for the care of dependants, could someone in your family help you in the short term?

Don't set off in pursuit of some hard-to-achieve ambition when time isn't on your side. Set yourself sensible goals – ones you stand a fair chance of realizing in the time you have available.

Multiple targeting

On Monday we looked at the importance of considering all the options. When a change of career is forced on you, it is a sensible idea to put as many irons in the fire as you possibly can. This will help prevent a situation arising where time has run out on you.

Most people in forced career changes have the advantage that they aren't hindered by fixed ideas. If you are in this situation, you will usually be prepared to consider anything within reason, and this flexibility can be played to your advantage. You can proceed with a number of ideas, not just one. This approach – called multiple targeting – not only increases your chances of success but also allows for the fact that some changes of career can take longer to realize than the time you have available (something you won't necessarily know in advance).

Stopgap measures

Multiple targeting is all well and good but what if it doesn't work? If none of the irons you've put in the fire comes up trumps in the time you have available, where do you turn to next?

When they reach this point, most people will grab at any lifeline that's offered. They'll take on temporary and/or low-skilled work just to shore up their finances. They become taxi drivers, waiters, couriers – you name it, the list is almost endless. This is the alternative job market, and finding a job in this market is a useful stopgap measure.

Fill-in jobs

Fill-in jobs play an important role in modern working life and having to take one should never be seen as an act of failure. On the contrary, having a source of income in a period of difficulty will help you to stay focused on your ambitions, whereas being out of work will force you down paths you wouldn't otherwise choose. Notably, having a job will enable you to see the opportunities offered to you for what they're really worth, rather than jobs you have to take because you have no choice.

The market for low-skilled work is one that most of us have tapped into at some points in our lives – often in our student days. What's interesting about this market, though, is that:

- it's always there
- the jobs aren't hard to get (no one is likely to put you through three interviews and a psychometric test if you're applying for a job as a cashier or janitor).

The difficulty, if there is one, is proving to employers that you're serious and not just using them as a stopgap. A mistake many people make when they're attacking the alternative job market is that they approach it in the same way as they attack the market for career jobs. The human resources manager quoted in the following box illustrates the point.

The wrong candidate

Here's what one human resources manager had to say about a candidate for a job in factory security.

'He'd been a manager in a large retail business which had closed down. His CV was very professional and contained a whole page of his management achievements. We could see straight away, though, that he'd been out of work for six months – meaning, pretty obviously, that he was applying to us because he was desperate. What did we do with his application? We turned him down, of course. We knew he would only stay with us for as long as it took him to get back into management again.'

Understandably, our HR manager is suspicious of the motives of someone applying for a job way below his capabilities. So what attributes would she like to see in a candidate for a job in security?

'Some previous experience would be useful but not essential. Ideally, we'd like someone who's smartly turned out, honest of course, reliable, good at dealing with people and who doesn't mind working long and unsociable hours.'

In the example above, the candidate's achievements in managing a retail business cut no ice with the human resources manager looking for a factory security guard. In fact, they put her off. What our candidate should have done instead was put together a new CV, leaving out his long list of achievements and bringing out in their place attributes that would identify him as good potential security guard material – for example:

- pride in appearance, good attendance record and willingness to work round the clock
- absence of criminal record
- experience in the uniformed services such as the armed forces
- a plausible explanation for why he is under-reaching, rather than leaving employers to draw their own conclusions.

Temporary work: using agencies

The problem of convincing employers that you're serious doesn't figure as prominently if the position you're applying for is a temporary one. The fact that you've got no interest in the job long term and your sights are cast elsewhere isn't going to bother them. The problem with temporary work is to make sure that it keeps coming – in other words, after you've finished your two-week assignment with one employer, you'll need to have another two-week assignment with someone else lined up.

Since the market for temporary work has largely been cornered by agencies, to 'keep the assignments coming' you need to build up a good relationship with the agency supplying you with work. In turn this means:

● always being straight with them
● not doing anything that might get you into their bad books.

With the first of these points, you can be quite candid with agencies about looking for a new career. Who knows – they may be able to help you. You can tell them that temping is just a stopgap.

To avoid getting in agencies' bad books, simply make sure that you never let them down. Not turning up for an assignment is, for example, a guaranteed way of getting on the wrong side of an agency. Not only will they have an irate client to deal with, but they will also have to find someone else at short notice.

The Trojan Horse technique

The Trojan Horse technique – worming your way into an organization in a lowly capacity and then attacking it from the inside – can be used in any situation where getting your foot in the door would otherwise prove difficult. To demonstrate how it works, let's look at the case of Craig.

Case study: Craig (part 1)

Forced by injury to give up his career in professional sport, Craig is now keen to get into sales, preferably in a big company that can offer him good prospects. Due to his lack of experience, however, he has no luck with his applications.

For three months Craig does temporary work for an agency – mainly van driving and warehouse work. One day the agency asks him to do a four-week assignment with a local large office equipment supplier. Interestingly, he applied for a sales job with the same company only a few months earlier but didn't get an interview.

The temporary job turns out to be filling in for someone who is off sick. It involves working in the mail room and carrying out a range of duties, including delivering and collecting mail from various offices. Sensing that he may be on to something if he can succeed in making a good impression, Craig does his best to please everyone. One of the offices he visits regularly is the sales office, where he soon gets to know the staff, including the manager, Wendy. He goes out of his way to be helpful and, on one occasion, gets Wendy some information she needs and makes sure that it's on her desk within half an hour of her asking.

Right from day one Craig strikes up a good relationship with Gurdip, the mail room supervisor. Gurdip is interested in sport and always keen to hear Craig's inside stories. Two weeks into the assignment, Gurdip asks Craig if he'd be interested in a permanent job in the mail room. The person who is off sick has decided not to return, so there is now a vacancy. Craig accepts immediately and Gurdip agrees terms with the agency for his transfer.

Over the next six months Craig continues to apply himself diligently to his tasks, to the point where Gurdip is effectively treating him as his number two. Excelling as a mail-room clerk isn't difficult for Craig, who realizes he is working way below his potential, on a salary little better than his earnings as a temp. His eyes are still firmly fixed on getting a sales job, even though he continues to have no joy with his applications.

Then, one day, he hears on the grapevine that someone in Wendy's office is leaving at short notice. Sensing that the time has come to get his face in the frame, Craig speaks first to Gurdip, explaining that, although he enjoys his job in the mail room, he has always had an ambition to get into sales. He then tells Gurdip what he has heard on the grapevine and that, if there is a vacancy in sales, he would like to apply for it.

Points to pick out from this case study so far are:

- Intentionally or not, Craig wormed his way into an organization with opportunities in the career he wanted to break into (sales). He had done this via a temporary job.
- Though the work was far below his capabilities, Craig set out from the start to be the star temp – effort that got him a permanent job.
- He identified the two key figures he needed to have on his side – Gurdip, his boss, and Wendy, the manager in sales.
- He worked hard on his relationships with both of them.
- He kept his ear to the ground and found out about the vacancy in sales.
- He then acted quickly (he sprung the trapdoor of the Trojan Horse) and made his intentions known to Gurdip.
- He spoke to Gurdip first.
- He was careful not to rub Gurdip up the wrong way by saying he was dissatisfied with the job in the mail room. In fact, he did the opposite and said he enjoyed it.

Case study: Craig (part 2)

During their talk, Gurdip tells Craig he respects his ambitions and understands his wish to realize them. He asks Craig if he has spoken to anyone else, to which Craig replies truthfully that he hasn't. Gurdip then says that perhaps it will be best if he (Gurdip) has a word with Wendy first, so he can lay the ground. Craig agrees.

Wendy is surprised to hear that Craig is interested in joining the sales team and confesses to Gurdip that, though she likes Craig as a person, she hasn't considered him as a possible candidate. One of her staff leaving at short notice has put her in a fix at a busy time and she has already asked HR to advertise for a replacement. Gurdip expresses concern when he hears this. Wouldn't Craig be put out if he saw the job being advertised? Wouldn't he feel he'd not been given a chance? Besides, wasn't it company policy to promote people from within where possible?

Wendy says she understands what Gurdip is saying but she needs people on the sales team with experience – people who don't need teaching the basics of dealing with customers and converting enquiries into orders. Craig, as far as she knows, doesn't have any sales experience so how could she possibly consider him? Gurdip, however, persists. He is worried, he says, about having to go back to Craig and tell him Wendy isn't even prepared to give him an interview. How will he react? How would Wendy react if she were put in the same position? Gurdip says he wouldn't be surprised if Craig puts in his notice and goes back to temping for the agency.

What we are seeing here is Gurdip fighting for Craig because he thinks highly of him (showing silent bargaining power) and feels it's right that he should be given a chance.

Case study: Craig (part 3)

After telling Gurdip she'll think it over, Wendy goes through the pros and cons of offering Craig the sales job. On the one hand, he'll have to be treated as a beginner and given training. On the other, he's already shown himself to be well motivated and reliable. What's more, he knows his way round and gets on with the staff. Wendy also sees how putting up the shutters to Craig will leave Gurdip in a difficult position. Worse still, Gurdip may feel resentful, leading perhaps to a cooling off of the good relationship she's always had with him.

Wendy picks up the phone. She's decided to tell HR to put recruitment of a replacement on hold. She'll interview Craig and lay it on the line to him that he'll have a steep learning curve to climb, just to see how he reacts. Providing she is satisfied he's got the commitment to see it through, she'll give him three months to prove himself – one way or the other.

As we saw earlier in the week, employers are more prepared to stretch a point when it comes to making opportunities for people internally. The barriers they would put up to external candidates are less in evidence for internal candidates – partly because of their silent bargaining power and partly because of what employers gain from allowing staff to develop and realize their ambitions. There are other forces at work here too – for example, it's easier to give a flat no to someone you don't have to pass in the corridor every day.

SUNDAY

MONDAY

TUESDAY

WEDNESDAY

THURSDAY

FRIDAY

SATURDAY

Summary

Today we have looked at forced career changes and the challenges you face when you find yourself in a no-choice situation. On the one hand, the clock is ticking against you and you can't afford to hang around. On the other, you're not burdened with too many fixed ideas about what you want to do and this can work to your advantage.

The lesson here is not to proceed with one change of career idea at a time but to run several alongside one another (multiple targeting). Using the flexibility that comes from not having many fixed ideas, you can keep a number of irons in the fire at once. In this way, you can make allowances for the length of time that career changes can take (sometimes more than the time you have available) and also for the general uncertainty of market conditions.

Finally, we looked at what you can do to buy more time by using the alternative job market. We also drew your attention to the Trojan Horse technique – working your way into an organization through temping or a menial job and then accessing it from the inside.

SUNDAY

MONDAY

TUESDAY

WEDNESDAY

THURSDAY

FRIDAY

SATURDAY

Fact-check (answers at the back)

1. When is time not on your side?
   a) When you're forced into making a career change ❏
   b) When your job starts to become boring ❏
   c) When you're over 55 ❏
   d) When you only want to work part time ❏

2. When you're under threat of redundancy, when is it best to start putting some irons in the fire?
   a) As soon as you've been given your redundancy pay-off ❏
   b) After you've taken some time out for a holiday ❏
   c) As soon as you feel you can face up to the hassle of applying for jobs ❏
   d) Straight away ❏

3. What is multiple targeting?
   a) Having more than one reason for choosing a new career ❏
   b) Writing off for more than one job ❏
   c) Registering with more than one employment agency ❏
   d) Pursuing a number of different career ambitions at the same time ❏

4. What is the Trojan Horse technique?
   a) Making false claims in your CV to make it easier to get interviews ❏
   b) Worming your way into organizations in menial jobs, then attacking them from the inside ❏
   c) Looking for opportunities in other countries ❏
   d) Playing for more time ❏

5. What is the alternative job market?
   a) Another name for the invisible job market ❏
   b) The market for low-skill and temporary work ❏
   c) Jobs in the black economy ❏
   d) Career-change opportunities ❏

6. When is it best to use the Trojan Horse technique?
   a) When your change of career is being forced on you ❏
   b) When you've got no money left in the bank ❏
   c) When getting your foot in the door is proving difficult ❏
   d) When you've tried everything else ❏

7. What is guaranteed to get you into the bad books of agencies that are providing you with temporary work?
   a) Failing to turn up for assignments ❏
   b) Not having a car ❏
   c) Asking to take a holiday ❏
   d) Telling them you're looking for a permanent job ❏

8. Why are employers suspicious of people who apply for jobs that are below their capabilities?
   a) They won't put much effort into the work ❏
   b) They haven't got the right motivation ❏
   c) They won't stay long ❏
   d) They're going to want too much money ❏

9. When you're out of work, what is the problem with taking a low-skill menial job?
a) You might get your hands dirty ❏
b) It will look bad on your CV ❏
c) It is beneath your dignity ❏
d) There isn't a problem ❏

10. Which of these is a forced career change?
a) Being made redundant ❏
b) Being told to change your career because of a serious medical condition ❏
c) Needing to earn more money to fund your lifestyle ❏
d) Getting a new boss you don't like ❏

SATURDAY

Taking a step down

Taking a step down – sometimes known as downshifting – is moving into a career that will involve less hassle, along with, perhaps, an opportunity to work fewer hours. Opting to work at something less demanding than previously is often a lifestyle choice, and it is one that people tend to make as they get older and/or when they are less financially dependent on the earnings they make from going to work.

We are all living and working longer, but the work we're doing now may not be what we want to go on doing as we get older. Stepping down and at the same time branching off into something completely different may therefore become an option more and more people will want to consider.

Today we will look at:

- what you need to bear in mind, including the financial ramifications of moving into a less demanding role
- what going back to being a beginner really means
- the options open to you when you are making plans to step down
- making a case to an employer
- networking as a way of finding what you want.

Issues to consider

Downshifting doesn't have to mean changing careers. You can, for example, stay in the same career but take on a role with fewer responsibilities and/or fewer hours. Today, however, we will be looking at taking the plan a step further and discussing not just how you can reduce your responsibilities but ways to take on a completely new career as well. There are several issues to consider.

Practical considerations

There is a practical point to bear in mind before you embark on any plan to move into a new career that is part of a bigger plan to step down. It is this: some careers call for long periods of training and/or time spent getting qualifications. So, for example, if you are looking for something for the next two or three years only, a career where it takes five years minimum to become proficient is hardly going to be suitable.

Financial considerations

People in middle to senior management positions who are in the later stages of their working lives are at an advantage over other career changers in that they are usually not short of funds. This arises from two factors:

- They are past the point where their expenditure is at its highest because their children have grown up and left home and loans such as the mortgage are paid off.
- They have enjoyed good earnings historically, and so they usually have savings and investments – funds on which they can draw.

Their financial projections will therefore look rather different from those arising from an earlier career change, where you have to consider:

- the salary you can expect to earn as a beginner
- how long it will take you to get up to the earnings of a proficient performer in your new career.

In other words, the cost of your career change is worked out on a diminishing scale over a period of years and this is what your financial plan must provide for.

When taking a step down, however, the idea is not to work your way back up to the dizzy heights you were once at. Reduced earnings will be a permanent feature that you'll need to take into account when working out the financial implications of going ahead with your project.

Exploring your options

If you're trying to get out of the rat race, one option for you to consider is to forget the idea of downshifting and simply go and find another job. Whatever you're finding intolerable or untenable about your present position may not be replicated elsewhere. Indeed, the diversity of the job market is such that you may be quite surprised by what's available. In short, you may be able to achieve what you are seeking by 'sideshifting', using the job market as a vehicle.

An option favoured by many would-be downshifters is to look for something part time. Either as part of a gradual winding-down process in preparation for retirement or to give you time to do other things, working for a limited number of hours a week has clear-cut appeal. What's more, the job market with all its diversity now has more opportunities for working part time than at any point in the past.

If you're looking for something part time, consider the following:

1 **Decide on the hours you want to work.**
This is not to invite you to be inflexible (e.g. 'I'll work from 9 a.m. to 10.30 a.m. on Mondays, 2 p.m. to 3 p.m. on Wednesdays and 1 p.m. to 4 p.m. on Thursdays'), for the simple reason that this will put you outside the pale as far as most job opportunities are concerned.

2 **Ask yourself what you're seeking to achieve.**
See what alternative patterns of work would be consistent with your aim. For example, if you want to have long weekends at your cottage in the country, blocks of Mondays/ Tuesdays/Wednesdays or Tuesdays/Wednesdays/Thursdays/ Fridays could equally be the answer for you.

3 **Check that you're engaging with reality.**
Keep your eye on the part-time vacancies in newspapers and professional journals and on websites. Talk to some recruitment consultants and seek their views on whether the hours you've selected fit in with what employers actually want.

Downshifting internally

On Wednesday we looked at how you might realize your career-change ambitions within the organization you work for. We saw that career changes are a lot easier to realize internally because you can exert leverage by bringing your silent bargaining power to bear. How does this apply to downshifting?

An employer faced with a request from one of its highly regarded senior managers to be allowed to go in a different direction might be prepared to go along with the idea. Alternatively, they might have some misgivings:

● Will the senior manager adapt to the new situation – or fail to adapt and go on to become a thorn in their side?
● Would it be fair on the person they'll have to report to?
● Could it be a cause of future problems?

It's important to be aware of the concerns that employers might have, which could cancel out the effect of your silent bargaining power. In short, be prepared for the internal route to downshifting not working. In any case, it may well be that you don't find the idea of downshifting in your own organization very appealing. The 'going back to being one of the boys or girls' may not be easy to achieve and it is understandable, therefore, why a lot of people aiming to downshift prefer to pursue their ambitions elsewhere.

Downshifting externally

Shopping the outside job market is what many would-be downshifters end up doing. They look for a new employer who will provide them with the opportunity they are seeking. However, as we saw on Thursday, the external job market is challenging for everyone, and downshifters will often have difficulty convincing employers that:

● they're serious
● they've thought through their ideas properly – including the financial ramifications.

What no employer wants is a new recruit who is going to be a short-term stayer. The cost and pain of having to go through a recruitment exercise all over again is something they will strenuously seek to avoid.

Downshifters, like all career changers, have the task of persuading employers that they're not just acting on a whim and that they've gone fully into all the implications of going back to being a beginner. Additionally, however, they have to convince employers that:

● they're not just looking for a port in a storm and that, once the heat is off, they won't start agitating for more money and/or be back on the job market applying for management positions again
● they won't have problems being on the receiving end of instructions, i.e. their new bosses won't find them awkward or difficult to deal with.

Convincing employers is all-important. They must be able to see that you've thought the whole thing through properly and understand that all you want to do is take a back seat, work fewer hours and use your skills and talents in a less demanding role. Again, this is a job for your CV and cover letters. It should also come across in any briefing you give to people such as recruitment consultants – spell it out to them and don't leave them to arrive at their own conclusions because they may not be the right ones. The same applies to interviews. If you're given an interview, seize the opportunity to set out your agenda.

Putting across your good points

Having calmed some of the bigger fears in employers' minds, the next task you face is to demonstrate the benefits of employing someone like you. Here are a few suggestions:

- You have got life experience (and plenty of it).
- You are stable.
- Your character is good.
- You won't be agitating for promotion.

In consequence, you will probably be quite happy going along and putting in a good day's work until the time comes for you to retire.

Again, this is a way of presenting yourself in your CV, your cover letter and your conversations with consultants. You are someone who is solid and reliable, someone who will introduce maturity and stability into the team. With certain employers, particularly those who have had bad experiences with younger people, you may just find you hit the right spot.

Professional networking

Finding step-down opportunities on the outside job market is still a tough call. You don't know the employers and they don't know you. They may, in fact, see you as someone who is carrying round baggage and give you a miss for this reason alone.

This is where professional networking can be invaluable. People who have spent a number of years in senior management positions have usually accumulated quite formidable networks of contacts. Tapping into these contacts is probably the best way of finding downshifting opportunities.

Case study: Luke

At 55 years old, Luke has a top job in the automotive components sector. He has put some money away and his pension is already secure. Now he is trying to escape from the stress of holding down this job and wants to do something different with his core skills, which are in sales. One of his contacts is Alan, who owns a small tool-making business (suppliers to Luke's firm). Alan tells Luke that he could do with someone working in his office – possibly part time – so that he can give more of his time to dealing with technical matters, an area of the business that Alan regards as his own personal forte. Luke thinks he will seize this chance.

Situations like the one in the case study above are typical of the way in which many people have downshifted by networking and tapping into contacts. They are dealing with people who know them and so the problem of convincing employers doesn't arise.

Don't forget to use networking as one of your methods of sourcing the job market for opportunities.

Summary

If you're one of those people in the fortunate position of being able to think about stepping down from the rat race and going off to do something completely different, you will have learned today that the world isn't waiting with open arms to welcome budding downshifters. You have a long way to go when you choose this option – particularly when it comes to getting would-be employers to take you seriously.

We have focused on what you need to bear in mind when you consider this step, and how to go about sourcing the right opportunities. The two most likely ways of achieving your ambition to go in this direction are by the internal route – using any leverage you can exert on your current employer to provide you with the opportunity – and by networking – accessing opportunities by using your contacts to help you break down the barriers.

Unfortunately, downshifting isn't necessarily the answer when life starts getting tough. An easier way out for most people, with far fewer financial implications, is simply to go and get another job.

SUNDAY
MONDAY
TUESDAY
WEDNESDAY
THURSDAY
FRIDAY
SATURDAY

Fact-check (answers at the back)

1. When you can't face any more of the stress you're getting at work, which of the following should you consider first?
   a) Downshifting ❑
   b) Asking to be made redundant ❑
   c) Resigning ❑
   d) Looking for another job ❑

2. When is downshifting an option for you?
   a) When you're getting older ❑
   b) When you feel you can't stand any more ❑
   c) When you find your job boring ❑
   d) When you can afford it ❑

3. When is putting together a financial plan for changing careers not necessary?
   a) When you've got plenty of money in the bank ❑
   b) When the plan is to downshift ❑
   c) It's always necessary ❑
   d) When you haven't got time ❑

4. What advantage is there in seeking to realize your downshifting ambitions internally?
   a) You can bring your silent bargaining power to bear ❑
   b) You can complain if your bosses won't help you ❑
   c) You won't have to face the bother of making job applications ❑
   d) There isn't any advantage ❑

5. What is the biggest problem downshifters face on the outside job market?
   a) Negotiating an acceptable salary ❑
   b) Getting employers to take them seriously ❑
   c) Loss of service-related benefits ❑
   d) Interviews that are time-wasters ❑

6. Which of the following would employers see as a plus point in a candidate who is downshifting?
   a) Ambition ❑
   b) Evidence they've given thought to their ideas ❑
   c) A brilliant CV ❑
   d) Having a wide range of management experience ❑

7. When looking for opportunities on the outside job market, what advantage does networking give you?
   a) You're dealing with people you know and who know you ❑
   b) You will be able to negotiate a better salary ❑
   c) The people you speak to will do you a favour without asking for anything in return ❑
   d) It's a guarantee you'll get the job ❑

8. What should you do if your partner is against the idea of you downshifting to take some of the stress out of your life?
a) Carry on anyway ❏
b) Find a partner who shares your thinking ❏
c) Take time out to talk it over ❏
d) As (c), and don't do anything until you reach agreement ❏

9. You want to work a four-day week so you can spend more time at your holiday home. Which of these should you do first?
a) Resign from your job so that you're free to look for something part time ❏
b) Put the proposal to your employer and see what answer you get ❏
c) See what the market for part-time jobs has to offer ❏
d) Ask for redundancy ❏

10. Which of the following is the biggest obstacle to downshifting?
a) Not being able to afford it ❏
b) Discouragement ❏
c) Being too old ❏
d) Not having enough confidence ❏

7 × 7

Seven trends for tomorrow

1 As the world continues to change, more and more people will have to face the challenge of moving into a new career at some stage in their working life.

2 As people have longer working lives, more will want to do something different as they get older.

3 As job markets become increasingly competitive, people will need to be more proactive in the way they source career-change opportunities.

4 Fearful of the cost implications of making bad selection decisions, employers will become even less inclined to take risks when it comes to hiring people. As a consequence, career changers may find themselves increasingly reliant on getting people they know to pull strings for them.

5 As businesses continue to drive down costs, there will be a tendency for more and more work to be concentrated into fewer and fewer pairs of hands. The opportunity this gives for amassing silent bargaining power is good news for people who have their eyes on realizing career-change ambitions internally.

6 Many people are carrying a burden of debt and this will affect them when they have to face the challenge of making a change of career.

7 The issue of social mobility will become a big driving force, as more people swap careers for no reason other than it may offer them a better chance to move up the ladder.

Seven top tips

1 Engage with reality. Stay engaged.
2 Explore ways of trying out a new career before committing everything to it. Sample the reality where you can.
3 Perfect the art of the possible. See what's there and, when there's an easy path, take it.
4 Stand by for employers to be sceptical. At interviews, expect tough lines of questioning on what's driving you.
5 Put the effort into shopping the invisible job market where competition from people with experience will be less of an issue.
6 Look at all the options when a change of career is being forced on you. Get as many irons in the fire as you can.
7 Know when the clock is ticking away. Don't procrastinate when the time is running out.

Seven things to do today

1 Make a list of your transferable talents.
2 Think of three ways you could add value to yourself by acquiring new skills (skills that would lend themselves to a new career).
3 Where applicable, talk to your partner. Make sure that you're both on the same wavelength.
4 Start a savings plan.
5 Check a few websites. See what they can tell you about the demand for new entrants into the career you are considering. Take note of any information about starting salaries and qualifications you will need.
6 Make a list of people to talk to (people in the know or people who may be able to provide you with some insight into the line of work you're considering).
7 Do a reality check. Drop any ideas that don't stand the test.

Seven things to avoid

1 Choosing to move into a line of work for which there is little
or no demand.
2 Putting all your eggs in one basket by considering only a
narrow range of options.
3 Getting cold feet at the critical moment.
4 Making threats when seeking to realize career changes
internally.
5 Failing to make it clear in your cover letter and CV that
you're seeking to make a change of career, and thus running
the risk of employers thinking you've applied for the wrong
job.
6 Getting discouraged when your job applications keep being
turned down.
7 Trying to change your career when all you need do is find
another job.

Seven surprising facts

1 The number of people who embark on a change of career without considering the financial implications.

2 How many people neglect to explore the opportunities for changing careers within the organization where they work. Far easier and less risky paths could be available to them without them realizing it. Often, all it takes is putting out a few feelers.

3 How long it can take some people to realize that they're viewing their choice of alternative career through rose-tinted spectacles.

4 How many people embark on plans to change their career without giving thought to whether or not there will be a job at the end of it.

5 How some people see a change of career as the answer to all the problems in their lives – and how often they find that it isn't.

6 That the most common cause of people failing to realize their ambitions is because they give up too soon

7 How many success stories start with someone having the guts to take a giant leap into the unknown.

Seven key messages

1 Manage risk as opposed to letting it frighten you.
2 Focus on your transferable talents. Think what else you could do with your bank of skills.
3 Keep on board people who are close to you. Don't let a career change get in the way of your important relationships.
4 See the exercise of silent bargaining power as the key to creating an internal path to a new career. See what leverage you have got and use it.
5 When seeking to make a career change internally make every effort to get the boss on your side. See the support of your boss as a critical factor in determining a successful outcome.
6 The job market will need convincing that you're serious. Face up to this challenge and think how you're going to overcome it.
7 Success is keeping going. Failure is giving up.

Seven good habits

1 Saving so the funds will be there when the need to change career arises.

2 Always having contingency plans in place. Being ready at all times for the unforeseen and the unpredictable. Spotting the warning signs when the future of your career is coming under threat.

3 Building an effective professional network – one that will be there when the need to make a change of career arises

4 Keeping your feet on the ground. Not letting flights of fancy take over when the need for careful consideration should be uppermost.

5 Adding value to yourself at every opportunity. Building up your silent bargaining power and the leverage you will be able to bring to bear on employers.

6 Not rushing into a change of career when time is on your side.

7 Being patient. Successful career changes can take a long time to realize.

Answers

Sunday: 1b; 2a; 3b; 4b; 5d; 6d; 7c; 8a; 9c; 10b

Monday: 1d; 2b; 3a; 4a; 5d; 6c; 7a; 8b; 9a or d; 10c

Tuesday: 1b; 2d; 3d; 4a; 5c; 6c; 7b; 8c; 9a; 10d

Wednesday: 1a; 2b; 3a; 4c; 5b; 6d; 7c; 8d; 9a; 10c

Thursday: 1d; 2b; 3c; 4a; 5b; 6c; 7d; 8d; 9a; 10c

Friday: 1a; 2d; 3d; 4b; 5b; 6c; 7a; 8c; 9d; 10b

Saturday: 1d; 2d; 3c; 4a; 5b; 6b; 7a; 8d; 9b; 10a